MARY
THE WOMB OF GOD

by

GEORGE A. MALONEY, S.J.

DIMENSION BOOKS

DENVILLE, NEW JERSEY

Imprimi Potest: Rev. Eamon Tavlor, S.J.
Provincial of New York Province
May 1, 1976

Published by Dimension Books, Inc.
Denville, New Jersey 07834

—Dedication—

To Cardinal Leon-Josef Suenens, who has done so much in his priestly life to promote true devotion to Mary the Mother of God.

ACKNOWLEDGEMENTS

Grateful acknowledgment is made to the following publishers who have so generously granted permission to reprint from their publications: Darton, Longman & Todd, Ltd. and Doubleday & Company, Inc., N.Y. for excerpts from *The Jerusalem Bible,* copyright 1966 by Darton, Longman & Todd, Ltd. and Doubleday & Company, Inc. All scriptural texts are from *The Jerusalem Bible,* unless otherwise noted. The poems of Bill Peffley are published with the permission of Balance House Publications, 101 E. Penn Street, Norristown, Pa. 19401. Caryll Houselander's poem: The Reed, is printed from the collection: The Flowering Tree (pg. 205-207) in: *The Mary Book,* assembled by F. J. Sheed, with permission of the publishers, Sheed and Ward, New York.

Finally great gratitude to Sister Joseph Agnes of the Sisters of Charity of Halifax for reading and typing this manuscript.

TABLE OF CONTENTS

INTRODUCTION

The age of Aquarius has come and gone. We are standing on a precipice watching a new era slowly unfold. This new age cannot be described adequately in terms of a new culture alone. Economic and social upheavals of past "systems," to be replaced by another one, will never exhaust the complexity or the simplicity of what is coming.

In the fourth century the rusty hinges that held together the tired, weary Roman Empire of the Caesars fell clanging to the ground. A new dynamic force swept through the land. Christianity, like a silent leaven, was raising humanity to a new level of community. The Church of Jesus Christ, His Body, was being formed again by those broken and contrite of heart. The little ones were being chosen to preach God's immense love for mankind. The weak ones of this earth were confounding the mighty. Although Constantine saw the sign of the conquering Cross in the heavens, the triumph would come first in the hearts of the meek and humble who lovingly embraced that Cross.

The Renaissance, the Age of Enlightenment and the Industrial Revolution fashioned the Western world into what Dostoevski termed "the great crystal palace." Man's mind had conquered over the heart and strove to materialize his dream of a thoroughly rational ordering of human life, based on Descartes' clear and distinct ideas.

Religiously, Western man lost the contemplative approach to God. Busy in his mind, fashioning God and the world according to his own designs, man moved farther and farther away from mystery and the inner world of symbols. He tends in modern society to worship a God of power. His rational conscious life is starved for the delicate, intuitive feminine. His psyche cries out for a wholeness, a union between his rational and intuitive powers.

THE WOMAN

The Prophet Isaiah had foretold the dawn of a new age:

> For now I create new heavens and a new earth, and the past will not be remembered, and will come no more to men's minds. Be glad and rejoice for ever and ever for what I am creating, because I now create Jerusalem 'Joy' and her people 'Gladness' (Is 65:17-19).

We are, I believe, on the beginning edge of this new age. The sign in the heavens replacing Aquarius is *Virgo-Mater*. The Virgin-Mother is the *Woman* entering into the pangs of childbirth. She is Mary-Church. Evil forces seek to swallow up her child as it is being born, but she will succeed and bring it to birth with a great progeny of other children.

Among Roman Catholics who maintained a constant devotion over the centuries to Mary as virginal Mother of God, there had developed a "masculine" approach to her.

Mariologists, theologians who specialized in building a theology around Mary's different prerogatives, battled each other in their attempts to formulate the key principle upon which all of their Mariological theses depended. As Mary was seen in her "absolute" role as Co-redemptrix and Mediatrix of all graces, she became separated from the Church and almost even from Christ Himself.

Through the influence of M. J. Scheeben a return to the biblical and patristic parallels between Mary and the Church developed very rapidly over the past two decades. Both Mary and the Church, as the early Fathers viewed them, were again seen in their virginal openness to receive the Word of God through the Holy Spirit, in their motherhood to bring forth, as the New Eve, a new progeny of regenerated children in a miraculous, virginal birth. As Mary gave birth to Christ, so the Church gives birth to the members of Christ's Mystical Body through the sacraments and through faith.

The virginal womb of Mary, St. Augustine asks, is it not Mother the Church? Grace mediated through Mary or the Church is always a participation in the incarnational, free-will act of Mary which is both maternal and spousal. Mary is the perfect type of regenerated humanity, the Church, in attaining its supreme fruit, through the feminine, maternal act of receiving Divine Life through the Holy Spirit.

A RETURN TO PENTECOST

In a Church that emphasized hierarchical authority, all too little attention was paid to the praying of Holy Scripture and openness to the charisms of the Holy Spirit.

We have seen a tremendous outpouring of the Holy Spirit and a freeing of God's people through the so-called charismatic renewal sweeping through the various Christian Churches.

It was on the first Pentecost, as Vatican II's *Constitution on the Church* points out, that ". . .Mary by her prayers imploring the gift of the Spirit, who had already overshadowed her in the Annunciation" (#59), was the mediator for the Christian community to receive the outpouring of the Holy Spirit.

Mary is the masterpiece of the Holy Spirit. That Holy Spirit overshadowed her all of her lifetime, infusing into her faith, hope and love. She is the perfect charismatic Christian as she, in love and faithful obedience, surrenders herself to serve God's Word.

Anyone who is of that same Holy Spirit will recognize her greatness. ". . .all generations will call me blessed" (Lk 1:48). Look at the very first book of the Gospel according to St. Matthew. The first spoken words in the Gospel of Jesus Christ are these:

> Joseph son of David, do not be afraid to take Mary home as your wife, because she has conceived what is in her by the Holy Spirit (Mt 1:20).

Protestants have for too long misunderstood Catholic devotion to Mary. They thought Catholics were either idolatrizing her to a peak of divinity or they were taking away from the unique mediatorship of Jesus Christ by allowing to Mary a cooperative role in our redemption.

We Catholics must confess that in some devotional writings Mary had been taken out of the Church and too much accent was placed on her exemplarity as a human model to be imitated in our daily lives. The biblical and liturgical revivals, along with the charismatic renewal and the hunger for deeper, contemplative prayer, are bringing us to a new appreciation of Mary, the Mother of God and our Mother too.

EASTERN CHRISTIAN CONTEMPLATION

And yet a new devotion to Mary with an accompanying, deeper understanding of Church as Spouse of Christ and our Mother is really not so new. It has always been present in the Eastern Christian Churches that first in 431 in the Council of Ephesus fought so strenuously for her title as *Theotokos*, Birthgiver of God. The early Fathers of the Church, under the illumination of the Holy Spirit, contemplated Mary as found in Holy Scripture. They could move freely from Mary to Church to the individual Christian and see the essential similarity because they were true contemplatives and true charismatic Christians. Such an understanding of the true essence of Mary, Church and individual Christians can be revealed to us by the Holy Spirit. It is not a speculative doctrine to be seized by the light of our own reasoning powers. It is an *experience* of becoming Mary-Church through the overshadowing of the Spirit of love.

This book is not, therefore, a speculative "Mariological" work. Nor is it a mere pious, devotional treatise. I have used much of the modern biblical and patristic scholarship to ground my writing in the objective Revelation of Scripture and Tradition. Yet I have tried to bring the head and the heart together. It is a humble attempt to present the mystery of Mary, drawing upon Holy Scripture and the inspirations of the early Church Fathers, along with insights from modern psychologists as Carl G. Jung, Erich Neumann and others, as well as modern theologians.

WOMB OF GOD

I have chosen the title: *Mary, the Womb of God*, to suggest the most primeval, archetypal experience that all of us human beings have had. We have all come into existence by first finding life in the womb of our mothers. Among the Byzantine theologians who developed a solid Marian theology, Mary and the Church and each individual Christian are wombs, "containers that contain the Uncontainable." She is the fertile, virginal Mother Earth that receives from the Spirit, not only at the Annunciation, but as a continued state of total surrender to God, the impregnation of God's Word.

The *womb* suggests to the Christian advancing in contemplative prayer the inner chamber that Christ spoke about (Mt 6:6) as the place where in silence we are to enter and adore the Heavenly Father in spirit and in truth. It is the focal point where, in man's most expanded awareness of the indwelling Holy Trinity, he meets the loving Lord and surrenders himself totally in loving submission.

In biblical language, it is our *heart* where Mary and we individual Christians must first receive the Word of God. Mary, in deep contemplative prayer, long before she received physically the Word as enfleshed in her womb, had received Him in her consciousness and in the deepest recesses of her unconscious. She was able to be God's Mother because she had allowed in utter active receptivity that God's Word would dominate completely in every facet of her being. Because Mary was totally woman, in her virginal faith and complete surrender to the Holy Spirit working within her from the first moment of her existence, she is the prototype of what every Christian must become.

We become true Christians through our *feminine* power of contemplation. We can only wait in joyful expectancy, but God is the Father, the one who first takes the initiative to let His Word enter into us. The womb of Mary is a dynamic archetypal symbol drawn from the Greek Fathers to express to us beyond a clear and distinct idea, even into the farthest reaches of our unconscious, the primeval urge that God has implanted into all of us when He fashioned us according to His image and likeness (Gn 1:26). Deep within us is an unquenchable hunger to surround, enfold, possess, hold, embrace, as a mother does her child in her womb, God's very own life-giving Word. From that inner possession of God's life we give birth to Jesus Christ in the events of our daily lives. Virginally by our total surrender in faith, hope and love, we conceive by the Holy Spirit and then maternally we give birth to God's Word and give that Word to others by our love and humble service shown to them.

It is my desire to share the gift of Mary, given to St. John at the foot of the Cross and to all of us Christians represented by the Beloved Disciple, the contemplative theologian, with my other Christian brothers and sisters.

May we all, under the guidance of the Holy Spirit, come to realize that "unless a man is born from above, he cannot see the kingdom of God" (Jn 3:3). One is born of a mother. Only the Spirit of Jesus can reveal to us the inner beauties of His Mother Mary and the gift she is to us. Only He can reveal to us the Church as His gift and our Mother too.

1

Mary the Contemplative

Some years ago I met Father Chrysostom, a Greek Orthodox monk, on Mount Athos. He lived in a hermitage with his disciple at the foot of Karoulia, the bleak rocky desert at the southernmost tip of this peninsula as it juts defiantly out into the blue waters of the Aegean Sea. On top, 250 feet above the waters, individual hermits rooted their one-room cells and sat like fearless eagles peering into eternity.

Because of his age, Father Chrysostom lived below the precipice. But I suspect he chose that spot also because of the cave that he made as his "holy place" to be alone with God. He could move directly from his cell into the natural cave carved out of the base of the mountain.

As he led me into this cool dark cave, he explained what it meant to him to pray there. "You see, it isn't very large. The ceiling and walls surround me like the arms of a mother. It is hard for me to describe the sense of God's warmth and intimacy that comes over me as soon as I enter into this cave."

Scattered man needs to "localize" himself when he wants to communicate with God. God, the incomprehensible, can never be comprehended, held in by any man-made concept or natural, spatial confinement. When man stakes off a sacred place and enters "inside," he enters into an archetypal experience that is not unlike his primeval experience of beginning life within the maternal womb.

I could understand now why the Greek Fathers were so fond of calling Mary the *Uroborus*, the womb of God. Mary, for all true Christian contemplatives, will always be the archetypal symbol of the ideal Christian in prayerful adoration and loving surrender to God almighty. The feminine element found in every human being, man or woman, can be described as the empty receptacle, as St. Irenaeus defines man before God. The *anima* is the vessel that opens to receive life. It is described as a circular movement of two walls that meet and enclose life itself.

It cannot take the aggressive initiative. It is pure receptivity, waiting to receive the male element that will begin the new life-process. It does not have it within itself to begin life. It must therefore wait expectantly.

It is typified by a joyful exuberance of expectancy. It hungers and thirsts to go beyond itself through communion that comes by a total surrender of itself as gift in love to the other.

Michaelangelo, in his famous Sistine-Chapel fresco depicting God's creation of woman, has captured something of this contemplative spirit in woman. Eve stands facing God her Creator, eyes focused upon Him with hands folded in loving adoration. God's face registers, along with the gesture of His hand, a look of tender love and hope. Into this receptacle God would pour the fullness of His Being.

It is no wonder therefore that Mary would be called

the *New Eve.* She, both by her spiritual and physical
virginity, would become God's womb out of which would
come the *New Adam.*

Tertullian (c.220) shows that into Eve, while still a
virgin, the word of the organizer of death crept,

> . . .likewise into a virgin (Mary) was introduced the Word of
> God, the builder of life, in order that that which through the
> same sex was lost, would through the same sex be restored and
> saved. Eve believed the serpent: Mary believed Gabriel. What
> that one (Eve) lost by believing the serpent, this one (Mary)
> corrected by believing.[1]

The Fathers liken the womb of Mary not merely to
the physical receptor of God's life, but to the intellectual
focal point, the "heart" where Mary listened and heard the
Word of God spoken through the Holy Spirit by the
message of the Angel Gabriel. St. Ephrem the Syrian
(c.373) has a number of references to Mary and Eve
describing the differences of "wombs." "Death entered
and spread through the womb, the ear (of Eve), so through
the ear, the new womb of Mary, life has entered and
spread."[2]

St. John Damascene also repeats this image of a
"hearing womb" by which Mary becomes the Mother of
God. "The conception was effected through the hearing."[3]
In his second homily on the Assumption, St. John Damascene writes: "But she, the truly blessed above all, (in
contrast to Eve) inclined her ear to the Word of God and
was filled by the operation of the Holy Spirit, and through
the Father's good pleasure announced by the archangel,
became pregnant."[4]

A UNIFYING PRINCIPLE

Here we see the basic belief that the early Church had
in regard to Mary's greatness. Theologians who write on
Mariology are continually discussing Mary's prerogatives in
their search for a unifying principle around which to hinge
all her prerogatives. Is it to be the Immaculate Conception
that holds the secret of Mary's perfections? Or is it the fact
of her divine maternity? Or does her glorious assumption
as a prototype of the Church's glorification in the *parousia*
as the Bride of Christ not give us this unifying element?

MARY – THE PERFECT CHRISTIAN

I would like to avoid such an approach and begin by
basing our deeper devotion to Mary on the fact that God
has given her to us as a realized type of the perfect
Christian. Mary, in her continued process of growing into a
greater fullness of grace, even in her glorified relationship
to Jesus Christ, to the members of His Body, the Church,
and to the whole created universe, stands as the model of
what we are destined to become by cooperating with
God's divine energies operating in our lives as they
operated in her life.

There is a danger in seeking one principle to the
exclusion of others as the fundamental touchstone. Whatever principle is chosen, such as the divine motherhood,
Mary and her prerogatives are all too often seen separated
from her dynamic growth as a human being. A static
representation of her physical motherhood of Jesus Christ
or of her spiritual motherhood of all Christians is given
that prevents any deeper growth in loving devotion

between us and the living Mary, Mother of God and our Mother.

THE ESSENCE OF CHRISTIANITY

If Mary is the prototype of the fully realized Christian, let us begin to see how, before she becomes the Mother of God, she unfolds as a seed does toward her fuller fruition. Mary becomes physically the virgin and Mother of God because she first consented to be spiritually dominated by God, her Lord and Master.

St. Luke tells us that Mary stored up all these things in her heart (Lk 2:50). Mary early in life contemplated God as the center of her life. She knew by experience in prayer that God had freely created her and breathed His divine life into her from the first moment of her existence. God's Holy Spirit was upon her much earlier than at the time of the Annunciation, impregnating God's Word in her heart.

Because she had, earlier than her visit to her cousin Elizabeth, all her life experienced the wonderful things that God had done in freely creating her and breathing His divine life into her, she was able to sing her *Magnificat* and proclaim that He who is mighty has done great things to her (Lk 1:46).

She knew in a more profound way than all other Christians that God was outpouring love, seeking entrance into her heart, and so she constantly surrendered herself in prayer and in her prayerful life to His holy designs. If God loved her so greatly, she also desired only to live for His love, to serve Him with every fiber of her being. Because Mary had contemplated and experienced God so deeply as

energizing love in her life, she was able to give her *fiat*:
"Behold, the handmaid of the Lord. Be it done to me
according to Thy word" (Lk 1:38).

Mary the contemplative accepted the gift of God's
love—His Holy Spirit—and in the power of that loving
Spirit she strove to love all mankind. God's power within
her drove her to aid her cousin Elizabeth in her pregnancy,
but only because it had driven her outwardly toward all
whom she met in her daily lfe at Nazareth before the
Incarnation.

What Mary contemplated as God dwelling actively
and lovingly within her she allowed to flow outwardly into
daily acts that reflected a person totally living "in" God.
Mary, not only in the Incarnation but also in her heart
through contemplation, yielded her whole being to serve
God's Word.

VATICAN II AND MARY

Vatican II brings this point out clearly in an attempt
to show that Mary's personal act of faith and her
cooperation continuously with the Holy Spirit were in a
process of growth in grace. It is this contemplative aspect
of Mary receiving God's continued communication
through the power of the Holy Spirit that Vatican II
wished to stress in order to claim Mary as the prototype of
the Church's act of fruitful faith, and that which each of
us individual Christians can and should imitate. Vatican II
put Mary's prerogatives of virginity and divine motherhood
back into the context of the Church. It stressed the
scriptural texts that show Mary's humanity and her need
to grow in grace.

Her glory is highlighted, not primarily because of her physical motherhood but because she heard and guarded God's word.

Lumen Gentium gives scriptural citations to confirm the praise of her Son on her behalf: "...He declared blessed (cf. Mk 3:35; Lk 11:27-28) those who heard and kept the Word of God, as she was faithfully doing (cf. Lk 2:29, 51)."[5]

This document portrays Mary as firstly in need of redemption. "Because she belongs to the offspring of Adam she is one with all human beings in their need for salvation."[6] It points out that devotion to Mary had not escaped some of the cultural limitations that did not place virginity always as a sign of wholeness, integrity and openness to the divine.

Vatican II takes pains to give the New Testament references that present Mary as a most human, growing person, reflective, loving, faithful. Jesus Himself in His references and relationships in the New Testament to Mary, His Mother, presents her as one who is faithful.[7]

Mary is uniquely worthy of our veneration precisely because, being intimately associated with the very source of grace, not only in the Incarnation but throughout all her human development, she responded by her active receptivity. She is what all human beings, male and female, must become. She is the first reflection anticipating what all Christians must become by grace, "made participators of God's very own nature" (2 P 1:4).

Mary is seen in the Vatican Constitution on the Church as *homo viator*, the pilgrim who contemplates by faith and obedience, hope and burning love, the saving work of God.[8]

FROM DARKNESS TO LIGHT

Mary like any Christian contemplative had to learn to walk by faith. We can believe that the great faith she needed to give her *fiat* to the message of the angel had been prepared by series of acts of faith developed throughout Mary's life as she contemplated God's message unfolding in her life before the Annunciation. We see her deep spirit of contemplative faith when we examine Lk 1:37, "For nothing is impossible to God". with the faith that was required of Abraham and Sarah (Gn 18:14). Mary had to walk all her lifetime by the same dark faith that St. Paul describes as a part of Abraham's surrender to God's promise (Rm 4:17-21). It was in a hope against all appearances that Abraham believed in God's promise to make him the father of many nations.

Mary becomes the mother of the faithful and the prototype of the Church and of each individual Christian by her virginal faith and total surrender to the Holy Spirit operating within her from the first moment of her existence.

And this surrender in faith to cooperate with the Holy Spirit is done through her personal acts. Mary is not a puppet. Nor is she one who begins to be the faithful handmaid of the Lord only at the time of the Annunciation. She evolved at each moment of her life as she contemplated God working in her life. "In an utterly singular way she cooperated by her obedience, faith, hope and burning charity in the Savior's work of restoring supernatural life to souls. For this reason she is a mother to us in the order of grace."9

MODERN PSYCHOLOGY AND THE FEMININE

Modern psychology describes the integrated human person as a harmonious blending of two psychic principles. The *animus* is the intelligible principle of analysis, which gives birth to critical reflection, to control and calculation. The *anima* is defined as the principle of relationships, of communion and unity.[10] L. Beirnaert insists that "It is the psyche, the anima, the soul that makes contact with God. . .and that is in a feminine relationship with God."[11]

The human person becomes a true Christian through his or her *feminine* power of contemplation. It is to open oneself with the totality of one's being to stretch in active receptivity toward the Transcendent God. It is to receive the love that God first has for man and thus, in contemplating God as immanently present within, to make a response in total obedience in love. Jesus appeals to the feminine in each of us when He says: "If you love Me, keep My commandments" (Jn 14:15).

Man proposes, woman accepts. There is an Arab proverb that says: "The man who is silent refuses. The woman who is silent consents." The feminine is characterized not merely by a receptivity, an acceptance, but more, by *response*, oblation, surrender, gift of self in loving obedience.

This is why Mary the contemplative is the archetypal symbol of the feminine in every human being. We come alive as Christians, the Church becomes the dynamic, living Body of Christ when we yield to the feminine in us. The womb of Mary powerfully describes to us in the deepest reaches of our unconscious that primeval hunger that God has implanted within all of us to circumvent, surround, enfold the wild, unpossessable, transcendent God.

Other religions such as Judaism and Islam have stressed the infinite abyss that separates man from God. It is, to quote Rudolph Otto's expression, the *mysterium tremendum*, the unfathomableness and unreachableness of God. No matter what man does, God always remains *beyond.*

Still other religions emphasize so completely the "inwardness" of God in all things that there is only the Absolute Self once man has moved beyond the *maya* or delusions of separation between God and man and the whole world.

MARY – THE SIGN OF CHRISTIANITY

But Mary stands as the sign of the distinct quality of the Christian Church, holding out to each human individual a synthesis of the perfect human being. She is the "place" where God's transcendence and immanence meet. She opens her whole being in silent contemplation of the awesome, majestic God and she hungers and thirsts to receive of His fullness. She embraces, womb-like, God's gift of Himself. She yields to His love by a return of love that proves itself by complete, docile obedience to Him. "Behold, the handmaid of the Lord. Be it done to me according to thy word" (Lk 1:38).

Mary as virgin is the archetype of the integrated human being. In her contemplation of God's supremacy, she experiences her creaturely poverty. She chastely desires to give her total being back to God. In complete obedience to God's wishes, she opens herself as virginal earth to God's fertility. She receives the divine Seed which

God the Sower casts into her. Meister Eckhart, the fourteenth-century Rhenish Dominican mystic, expressed this archetypal symbol of woman found in all human beings in these bold words:

> For man to become fruitful, he must become a woman. Woman! That is the most noble word that can be addressed to the soul, and it is far nobler than virgin. That man should conceive God within himself is good and in this predisposition he is a virgin. But that God should become fruitful in him is better. For to become fruitful through the gift received is to be grateful for the gift. And then the intellect becomes a woman in its gratitude that conceives anew.

The symbol of woman suggests a movement inward, toward creating life. The peak of womanhood touches our human transcendence and excellence and becomes the best in us when woman stands for one who completely and totally accepts life from the Other, unites in loving service to that new life as now a sign of her communion with the Beloved.

UNION BETWEEN CONSCIOUSNESS AND THE UNCONSCIOUS

Carl G. Jung in his book: *Answer to Job* discusses the importance of Mary as the archetypal symbol of the feminine in all human beings. He laments the fact that Protestantism has rejected devotion to Mary and thus, losing the feminine and appreciation for the interior, contemplative life, it has become a "masculine" form of Christianity.[12] Because of Catholic devotion to Mary, there is, according to Jung, the possibility of a union between consciousness and the unconscious.

But if the individuation process is made conscious, consciousness must confront the unconscious and a balance between the opposites must be found. As this is not possible through logic, one is dependent on symbols which make the irrational union of opposites possible. They are produced spontaneously by the unconscious and are amplified by the conscious mind. . . .It is only through the psyche that we can establish that God acts upon us, but we are unable to distinguish whether these actions emanate from God or from the unconscious. . . .Consequently, it does not seem improbable that the archetype of wholeness occupies as such a central position which approximates it to the God-image. . . .Faith is certainly right when it impresses on man's mind and heart how infinitely far away and inaccessible God is; but it also teaches his nearness, his immediate presence, and it is just this nearness which has to be empirically real if it is not to lose all significance. . . .The religious need longs for wholeness, and therefore lays hold of the images of wholeness offered by the unconscious, which, independently of the conscious mind, rise up from the depths of our psychic nature.[13]

Mary as virgin and mother becomes the archetype of the feminine contemplative spirit that lies as the integrating, healing force between our human consciousness and our unconscious. In the symbol of Mary as virgin we see ourselves as individuals, and the Church, the community of individuals brought into unity by the Spirit of Jesus, possessing a basic potential for wholeness, a healing unto full life, a happiness that flows from the fulfillment of this potential for greater being. Virginity on this primeval level is man opening himself to God's initial love in total acceptance. It is the letting go of our lives in faith and child-like trust in God to let Him have full centrality in our lives.

In the symbol of Mary as Mother of God we see

ourselves realizing the basic hunger for God in our loving response to God. When we not only consent to receive God but actually bring Him forth in a life that is a continued response in loving obedience to God, then we too become mothers of God. The Holy Spirit effects an impregnation of God's Word within us. Man's motherhood of God is shown by the fruit of the Spirit: love, peace, joy, gentleness, kindness, patience, forbearance (Ga 5:22). Motherhood of God's Word is contemplation in action. The virgin, waiting, reflecting, listening, becomes the mother, responding.

MARY THE CONTEMPLATIVE

But what makes Mary not only the physical but also the spiritual virgin and mother of God throughout her whole life, before and after the Incarnation, at the foot of the Cross and among the disciples receiving the outpouring of the Holy Spirit on Pentecost is that she always was a contemplative.

Mary is the fully realized Christian because she constantly contemplates the Word of God. God has created all of us "according to His image and likeness" (Gn 1:26) and calls us to an ever-increasing union with Him through contemplation of His Word in us and in the whole world. The end of our life is to contemplate God. St. Paul phrases it in terms of Jesus Christ. "There is only Christ: He is everything and is in everything" (Col 3:11).

In the Christian East where contemplation is esteemed, the feast of Mary's presentation in the Temple is a witness on the part of Eastern Christians, not so much to an historical event but rather to a symbol that shows us

that our Christian end is tied to Mary's complete dedication to serve God. Mary is the fulfillment of Israel moving
toward the Heavenly Jerusalem in total surrender and
loving submission. This feast relays to us something of
Mary's child-like enthusiasm and burning desire to live a
life of total concentration on God and in His service.

Mary the contemplative in her *Magnificat* opens to us
the level of mystical union she had attained. Before the
Word that is forming within her womb, but that had
already over all her youthful years of silent contemplation
received birth in her heart, Mary sees herself only in
humble service to exalt God's glory and mercy toward His
people. She brings us to the opposite pole from the *I will
not serve* and *you will be like gods* of the first sin of angels
and of man.

This burst of loving service and humility toward the
awesome God calls us to a similar contemplative experience of God's allness in our lives and our dignity and joy in
surrendering, loving service.

My soul proclaims the greatness of the Lord
and my spirit exults in God my saviour;
because He has looked upon His lowly handmaid.
Yes, from this day forward all generations will call me blessed,
for the Almighty has done great things for me.
Holy is His name,
and His mercy reaches from age to age for those who fear Him.
He has shown the power of His arm,
He has routed the proud of heart.
He has pulled down princes from their thrones and exalted the
    lowly.
The hungry He has filled with good things, the rich sent empty
    away.
He has come to the help of Israel His servant, mindful of His
    mercy

—according to the promise He made to our ancestors—
of His mercy to Abraham and to His descendants forever
(Lk 1:46-55).

THE PRAYER OF THE HEART

St. Luke must have known Mary and her prayer-
fulness either by direct communication with Mary herself
or from information given him by those who knew Mary
intimately, especially St. John the beloved disciple to
whom Mary was entrusted by Christ on the cross. Twice
St. Luke indicates Mary's contemplative spirit. At Bethlehem she reflects on the words of the shepherds. "As for
Mary, she treasured all these things and pondered them in
her heart"(Lk 2:19).

Again, Mary's attitude toward all the events of the
hidden life at Nazareth is summarized by the similar
statement: "His mother stored up all these things in her
heart" (Lk 2:51). Mary's heart, that focal point of deepest
personalized consciousness, was always centered on Jesus
the Word. She does not accept to give birth to God's Word
for her own aggrandizement. She pondered every happening of her Son in the light of the Holy Spirit. What
contemplative pondered with clearer insights than Mary
the Old Testament prophecies about the coming of the
Messiah and understood them to be fulfilled in the
historical Jesus of Nazareth?

At the wedding feast of Cana Mary shows forth the
fruits of her contemplative life. What depths of meaning
were conveyed to herself and Jesus in those simple words:
"Woman. . .my hour has not yet come" (Jn 2:4). She
would hear that same title of *woman* addressed to her as
Jesus hung dying on the Cross: "Woman, this is your son"

(Jn 19:26). In Jesus' apparent rejection of Mary's implicit request to perform a miracle, the contemplative heart of Mary must have understood more than what the mere words would imply. She had contemplated herself in total service of God's Word. As Christ begins His public ministry, He is also calling Mary away from merely her maternal role as performed at Nazareth to assume an intimate role ("What is this to me and to thee?")

But yet Jesus does manifest His glory by performing the miracle on Mary's request. Mary the contemplative comprehended much when she ordered the servants: "Do whatever He tells you" (Jn 2:5). She must have realized that in His manifestation of divine power at Cana and in the ignominy of the *kenosis* on the Cross through which He would enter into the full glory (Ph 2:6ss) of His resurrection, she was to have a role to play, far greater than that of being physically the mother of Jesus.

After having pondered in her contemplative heart all the things that happened to her Son and all the prophecies concerning the coming Messiah found in the Old Testament, Mary heard this word *"Woman"* at Cana and at the foot of the Cross and she knew she was to be the *woman* of the new creation, mother of all born by the life (the new wine) of her Son in them.

St. Epiphanius (+403), in keeping with the patristic, mystical understanding of Scripture beyond the merely historical sense, captures the parallel between Mary and Eve as two mothers of the living.

It is she (Mary) who was intended through Eve. Eve it was who received in figure the name of Mother of the living. For Eve had been called this after she had heard the words 'You are dust and unto dust you shall return.' It was an amazing thing that, after she had sinned, she should receive this magnificent name. We must not see only the sensible reality that from her the whole human race on earth would take its birth but according to the truth that it is Mary from whom life itself would be born for the world because it was she who gave birth to a life and thus Mary became Mother of the living. It is then in figure that Mary has been called Mother of the living.[14]

STABAT MATER

Mary the contemplative must have reached her peak of mystical union with Jesus Christ by experiencing the terrifying dark night on Calvary. She had said her *fiat* long ago. Now her virginal acceptance and maternal response reach their fullest expression.

St. John the Evangelist, who stood beside Mary at the foot of the Cross, knew as Mary did that Jesus' *hour* with its promised victory over the Adversary would take place there. John wrote: "Now is the judgment of this world; now will the Prince of this world be cast out. And I, if I be lifted up from the earth, will draw all things to myself" (Jn 12:31-32).

When she heard Jesus' words: "Woman, this is your son" (Jn 19:26), Mary must have recalled the Cana wedding when she first heard herself addressed as *woman*. His hour had come. Because of her mothering of Him into His human existence that brought Him unto His transitional form unto glory and victory over the Kingdom of Satan, she was being called now into a new relationship with Jesus Savior.

Many commentators see evidence in St. John's selection of words in John 19:26 that he was linking up Mary with the *Woman* of Gn 3:15:

> I will make you enemies of each other:
> you and the *woman*,
> your offspring and her offspring.
> It will crush your head
> and you will strike its heel.

Mary's presence near to the crucified Savior leads her into a new relationship both in regard to her Son and the children born of the Spirit of Jesus. She had been asked to surrender her "possession" of her physical Son when He called her *Woman* at Cana and began His ministry. She lived out that suffering that climaxes on Calvary. Yet she too enters into His total oblation to the Father and breaks through to a new dimension as *Mother of living.*

Using the word *woman*, St. John links up the prophecy of Gn 3:15, the *Woman* participating in the defeat of the Serpent; the *Woman* at Cana (Jn 2:4); and the *Woman* standing at the foot of the Cross (Jn 19:27).

WOMAN, BEHOLD THY SON

Mary received on Calvary a new relation to Jesus Christ. Beyond the evident solicitude of Jesus to provide support and protection for His mother by entrusting her to His beloved disciple, Jesus calls Mary to look upon John, as so many of the early scriptural commentators noted, as now a son representing all the children of Mary's new motherhood. Mary the contemplative grew in her union with Jesus Christ at the foot of the Cross to realize that she is now mother to Christ's risen Body, the Church.

One of the medieval commentators on this Johannine text, Gerhoh of Reichersberg, expressed this common understanding of Mary's new motherhood received at the foot of the Cross.

> Next to her son, Mary is the beginning of the holy Church. For she is the mother of the apostle, to whom it was said: 'Behold thy mother.' But what is said to one, can be understood as spoken to all the apostles, those fathers of the new Church. And moreover because Christ had prayed for all those who should receive the faith through those same apostles, that they should all be one, so the same words can be understood of all the faithful who love Christ with all their hearts. What was said to the one, to John who so loved him and whom Christ loved more than all the others, can be applied to all who love him.15

MARY THE WOMAN TOWARD OTHERS

It was at Pentecost that Mary received an outpouring of the Holy Spirit that enabled her, more than any of the Apostles, to understand the universal love of her Son and Savior for all human beings. By the Spirit of Jesus Christ she burned to surrender herself even more completely to serve His Body than she had done at Nazareth or at the foot of the Cross.

With new awareness of her love for all God's children, she understood more deeply her universal role as Mother of the regenerated race of mankind. If St. Paul could shout out: "I live now, not I, but Christ lives in me" (Ga 2:20), how much more did Mary realize after Pentecost and continue to grow in that realization in her glorified state that she is one with Jesus. His love is her love for all of God's children. She lives now with ever-increasing grace, i.e. the indwelling, loving, uncreated energies of the Trinity abiding within her and energizing her to be present in loving service to each person in need.

Mary the contemplative becomes the loving servant of the Lord. Love received makes it possible for her to give of that love. *Contemplata aliis tradere*—to share with others the riches contemplated. From feminine to masculine, a womb that receives rich life opens to release that life, Mary becomes for us the completely realized, integrated human being. The contemplative in action is the virgin-mother of the Word of God, receiving and sharing that Divine Life with the whole world.

THE REED

She is a reed,
straight and simple,
growing by a lake
in Nazareth:

a reed that is empty
until the Breath of God
fills it with infinite music:

And the breath of the Spirit of Love
utters the Word of God
through an empty reed.

The word of God
is infinite music
in a little reed:

It is the sound of a Virgin's heart,
beating in the solitude of adoration;
it is a girl's voice
speaking to an angel,
answering for the whole world:

It is the sound of the heart of Christ,
beating within the Virgin's heart;
it is the pulse of God,
timed by the breath of a child.
The circle of a girl's arms
has changed the world—
the round sorrowful world—
to a cradle for God.

She has laid Love in His cradle.
In every cot,
Mary has laid her Child.

In each comes Christ;
in each, Christ comes
to birth;
comes Christ from the Mother's breast
as the bird from the sun
returning—
returning again to the tree he knows,
and the nest,
to last year's rifled nest.

Into our hands
Mary has given her Child:
heir to the world's tears,
heir to the world's toil,
heir to the world's scars,
heir to the chill dawn
over the ruin of wars.

She has laid Love in His cradle,
answering for us all:
"Be it done unto me:"
The Child in the wooden bed,

the light in the dark house,
the life in the failing soul,
the Host in the priest's hands,
the seed in the hard earth,
the man who is child again—
quiet in the burial bands
waiting his birth.

Mary, Mother of God,
we are the poor soil
and the dry dust;
we are hard with a cold frost.

Be warmth to the world;
be the thaw,
warm on the cold frost;
be the thaw that melts
that the tender shoot of Christ
piercing the hard heart,
flower to a spring in us.

Be hands that are rocking the world
to a kind rhythm of love;
that the incoherence of war
and the chaos of our unrest
be soothed to a lullaby;
and the round and sorrowful world
in your hands,
the cradle of God.

                              Caryll Houselander

2

Mary Virgin

One of the great achievements of the Western world is the movement of man toward greater and greater consciousness. Science with its sophisticated technology has placed man on the moon and allowed us to be in immediate contact through satellite transmission with happenings of our fellow beings in any part of the world. Presence to another, a product of expanded consciousness, is more important than space or time.

And yet such possibility toward even greater expanded consciousness, toward "being present to the other" has not been actualized as one might expect. Erich Neumann, in tracing the development of human consciousness, laments the fact that the West has identified itself with the masculine at the expense of the feminine. This is seen in the symbols the West values: science, rational proof, technology, aggressiveness, laissez-faire, rugged individualism, etc. It is the triumph of the head over the heart. He writes:

> To become conscious of oneself, to be conscious at all, begins with saying 'no' to the *uroborus*, to the Great Mother, to the

unconscious. And when we scrutinize the acts upon which consciousness and the ego are built up, we must admit that...they are all negative acts. To discriminate, to distinguish, to mark off...these are the basic acts of consciousness. Indeed, experimentation as *the* scientific method is a typical example of this process: a natural connection is broken down and something is isolated and analyzed....As against the tendency of the unconscious to combine and melt down, to say to everything *'tat twam asi'* 'that art thou'...consciousness strikes back with the reply 'I am not thou.'[1]

Neumann defines the *animus* or masculine as "focused consciousness" while the *anima* or feminine is the "diffuse awareness." The feminine is open, receptive, waiting expectantly for new richness in order to receive of it and become ever more its true self. The feminine was exalted by Jesus Christ when He preached:

Unless a wheat grain falls on the ground and dies, it remains only a single grain; but if it dies, it yields a rich harvest. Anyone who loves his life loses it; anyone who hates his life in this world will keep it for the eternal life (Jn 12:24-25).

ETERNAL FEMININE

For Christians, Mary will always be the sign of the eternal feminine. She stands as the fulfillment of all human beings. She is *Sophia*, the Wisdom of God lived out in the truth of the Holy Spirit. She cries out to all of us in her strong but delicate, tender but enduring obedience to God's holy will that we become truly human first by becoming feminine.

Only when we realize the Mary in us, the feminine openness to God's free gift of Himself into our lives, do we begin to be what God destined us to become. The feminine in us, as in Mary, develops within us and leads us to fully integrated personalities only when we can let go of the controlled consciousness we hold over our lives and surrender in ontological poverty to God's gift of grace.

VIRGINITY OF MARY

We have all read too many books on Mary that treated her virginity and motherhood in static, even biological terms that consequently closed us from Mary's deeper, archetypal relation to us as a sign of the enriching feminine in our relations toward God. Before we can understand Mary's virginity in a fuller sense with greater enrichment for our own spiritual growth, let us recall the Church's traditional teaching about Mary's virginity as found in Scripture and in the apostolic tradition.

The Nicene Creed, recited by most Eastern and Western Christians as the basic symbol of faith, professes: "and in Jesus Christ. . .conceived by the Holy Spirit, born of the Virgin Mary. . ." Eastern Orthodoxy and Roman Catholicism have for 2,000 years maintained an unwavering faith in the virginal birth. This means that Mary, as St. Luke records in his Gospel (Lk 1:35), conceived her Son Jesus Christ through the power of the Holy Spirit without any intervention of an earthly father.

A VIRGIN IN BIRTHGIVING

In the first half of the third century, Christian writers did not feel any special attraction to maintaining that Mary preserved her physical virginity in giving birth. It is not a grave question for Irenaeus, Clement of Alexandria and Origen who believed she gave birth in a most natural manner. Still this was not incompatible with her virginity. Writers in the fourth century, such as Athanasius, Cyril, Epiphanius, Basil and Gregory of Nazianzen. seemed to think it was not a very important issue. Basil insists simply that Mary never ceased to be a virgin and mother. Gregory of Nyssa, however, insists that Mary participated in no sensual pleasure before and no pain or labor during birthgiving. His disciple, Amphilochius of Iconium, insisted that "the virginal gates were not opened at all." The manner of Christ's birth was in a fashion inexpressible.

After the Council of Ephesus (431) that solemnly decreed that Mary was truly the Mother of God, her sanctity was exalted as well as her virginity before, during, and after. It is indeed difficult to understand today just what virginity in birthgiving would mean or also its value. Without defining its meaning in the mind of the patristic writers or later councils, we can understand the faith in the Church that moved ever more to a greater awareness that Mary, being under the power of the Holy Spirit not only in her conception but from the first moment of her existence, would not have been subjected to the curse that God imposed on the disobedient Eve: "I will multiply your pains in childbearing. You shall give birth to your children in pain" (Gn 3:16). A woman touching birth and at the same time so closely death itself, not enjoying the awareness of being under the power of the Holy Spirit as Mary was, must experience more pain than Mary. We can say in this matter, therefore, that the faith of Christians from the fourth century to the present posits some intervention of God allowing Mary to have experienced more joy than pain, more of humble service to God than a

bewildering panic of fear. Virginity in this case would not be so concerned with a biological examination of how Mary brought forth Jesus from her womb but rather would touch her virginal consciousness that she was bringing forth her child as a total gift from God. In some way she grew in her virginity of self-surrender to God to serve His Word in that act of birthgiving.

A VIRGIN AFTER

The question of whether Mary and Joseph had conjugal relations after the birth of Jesus has been a disputed problem among Christians throughout 2,000 years. In Matthew's Gospel there seems to be an implication that Jesus had brothers. "Is not his mother the woman called Mary, and his brothers James and Joseph and Simon and Jude? His sisters, too, are they not all here with us?" (Mt 13:55).

The Proto-Evangelium of James presents Joseph as a widower, having children by his former wife and too advanced in years to have conjugal relations with Mary. This solved the difficulty in a very naive manner which detracts from any deep personal love between Joseph and Mary and makes him a "guardian" rather than a Jewish husband. But the strong tradition is on the side of Mary's freely choosing to remain a virgin after giving birth to Jesus. Origen was one of the earliest writers to give expression to the popular Christian belief: "No one whose mind is correctly on Mary would claim that she had any child save Jesus." The deep-rooted persuasion of her continued virginity comes from the belief that through the

Incarnation her body, like a temple, was irrevocably consecrated to the Holy Spirit and to God's Word.

Modern biblical exegetes place great emphasis today on the dynamics of a growing awareness of what God was asking of Mary in her consent to become the mother of God.[2] Mary and Joseph had been betrothed, a formal legal transaction in which Mary's father would have handed her over to Joseph as her legal husband before the Law. They had not cohabited yet, hence Mary's question to the angel: "But how can this come about, since I am a virgin?" (Lk 1:34). Knowing the Jewish idea of marriage as geared toward having children, we need not think that Mary had made an irrevocable promise to God to be always a virgin in marriage.

Knowing she was a virgin at the Annunciation, she rightly wondered how she was to be the mother of the Messiah. She had been conceived without sin. She grew daily in understanding the meaning of Scripture. Her desire to surrender to God completely, with perfect submission to His decrees in all matters, grew daily also. Mary's virginity should not be conceived of in a static manner but in the dynamics of a day by day searching to do God's will unconditionally.

Mary, married to Joseph, had only one virginal desire: to serve God as *He* wished. If this meant to lead a normal married life with Joseph, so be it. Once God spoke to her with His message that He wanted her to be the Mother of the Messiah, she moved a step closer to know how God wanted her to live out her surrender. Christian virginity was born at the moment when Mary was illumined by the Holy Spirit to surrender herself psychically and spiritually in her *fiat* that she also understood as embracing perpetual virginity.

A THEOLOGY OF VIRGINITY

We can all readily admit to an embarrassment at
reading statements of Mary's virginity written by church
writers heavily imbued by a Platonic or Manichaean
philosophy that would disparage Christian marriage as
something quite a bit less perfect than the perfect state of
angelic virginity. Karl Rahner proposes a much needed
theological basis for appreciating Jesus' virginal birth from
Mary and hence the true beauty of her virginal surrender
to God throughout her whole life. Jesus Christ is born
without an earthly father because He always existed as the
Word of His heavenly Father from all eternity.[3]

God gradually revealed His condescending mercy, His
Hesed Covenant, to His people. Over and over in the Old
Testament, God shows His free, gratuitous love and
election, irrespective of any personal or national merits on
the part of His prophets or the nation of Israel. When "in
the fullness of time" Jesus Christ was born of Mary, God's
condescending mercy became incarnate. His glory, the
Shekinah, now radiated from this Son of Mary. Because He
took His life-spring from God His Father, He would not
take any beginning of God's mercy incarnate from the side
of man, the aggressor. In human conception the woman
receives; the man begins the process. But in the Incarnation, the initiative was totally on God's part. "God loved
the world so much that He gave His only Son. . ."
(Jn 3:16).

> But God loved us with so much love that He was generous
> with His mercy: when we were dead through our sins, He
> brought us to life with Him and gave us a place with Him in
> Heaven, in Christ Jesus. This was to show us for all ages to

come, through His goodness toward us in Christ Jesus, how
infinitely rich He is in grace. Because it is by grace that you
have been saved, through faith; not by anything of your own,
but by a gift from God; not by anything that you have done,
so that nobody can claim the credit. We are God's work of art,
created in Christ Jesus to live the good life as from the
beginning He had meant us to live it (Ep 2:4-10).

God's mercy incarnated in Jesus Christ would have
His Father from above, not born of flesh or the will of
man, but of God. There is a very important exegesis and
recension tradition that gives us St. John's testimony of
the virginal birth in his Prologue. Verse 13 of the Prologue
is usually translated, especially in the traditions following
the Vulgate lineage, as: " 'But to all who did accept Him,
He gave power to become children of God...who *were*
born not of blood or the will of the flesh or the will of
man, but of God" (Jn 1:12-13). The New Jerusalem Bible
translates this phrase according to a very ancient version
known in the early church Fathers' commentaries on this
passage:

> But to all who did accept Him, He gave power to become
> children of God, to all who believe in the name of Him, who
> *was* born not out of human stock or urge of the flesh or will of
> man, but of God Himself.[4]

Such a translation would confirm the virginal birth as
expressed in Mt 1:16, 18-23 and Lk 1:26-38. The most
ancient authorities as Irenaeus, Tertullian and Augustine
use this translation which would give an important witness
of St. John to the virginal birth. Jesus was, according to
this interpretation, born from above; there was no "will of
man" but only "of God Himself" that was the aggressive,

creative force bringing Him into our existence. The action was completely on the part of God.[5]

THE VIRGINAL CHURCH

Mary understood by the power of the Holy Spirit, each day of her life before the Incarnation, that everything about her came from God as a gift: her existence, her loved ones, the beauties of nature around her, the whole world that thrilled her heart and made her often shout out with joy: "My soul magnifies the Lord; my spirit rejoices in God my Savior. . .because He who is mighty has done great things to me!" (Lk 1:46-49). She knew, more than any other human being, that she was an empty receptacle that was constantly being filled by God's gifts, His graces. What she experienced in her soul and spirit, she also experienced in her body. God touched her profoundly and by grace made her realize she was total gift on every level. She wanted to surrender herself in a willing submission to belong in the totality of her being to God. What she experienced in prayer, she wanted to live in a concrete, lived manner. For this reason she was total virgin, always returning herself, body, soul, spirit, her whole being completely to God.

Because she was not only spiritually but also physically a virgin in a way that could have been witnessed to, especially to St. John the Evangelist and the other Apostles and early members of the Christian community, she stands as the archetype of the Church in the thinking and prayer life of the early Church.

The Church, like Mary, receives all of its unique meaning as total gift of grace from God. There is nothing from this world. The Church is the Body of Christ, meant to form His life in its members, but through grace, life from above, from God and not "of the will of man."

VIRGINS FOR CHRIST

All Christians are to imitate the integrity of Mary in heart and mind, to recognize God as the ultimate source of all life and to surrender to His primacy. It means to develop the faith and obedience of Mary in surrendering devotion and love to God in His gifts of grace and charisma.

Yet in the Christian Church from earliest times, as St. Paul clearly shows and Jesus Christ preached: "there are eunuchs who have made themselves that way for the sake of the Kingdom of Heaven. Let anyone accept this who can" (Mt 19:12). St. Paul practised his preaching: "An unmarried man can devote himself to the Lord's affairs, all he need worry about is pleasing the Lord" (1 Co 7:32).

Virginity as a fixed state of life freely chosen by Christian virgins is a charism given by God. Much like the infusion that Mary received from the Holy Spirit to witness to God's complete, condescending, graceful love, such virgins not only yield themselves to God in faith and obedience as all Christians must do but they also witness to the primacy of grace and the ultimacy of God's Kingdom in a physical surrender of themselves. They become a sign of the future Kingdom when this finite earth will be transformed into the *parousia* of the glorious Body of Christ. But they also attest that God's power has already begun to do this new thing by His grace in their present pilgrim lives.

Such virginity, therefore, has an apostolic thrust. Sacrifice for the Kingdom is unto greater life of service to others in self-giving, but also to draw others to imitate their total dedication to God.

VIRGINAL FREEDOM

Mary in her virginity, and those who imitate her, move away by the grace of the Holy Spirit from any "worldly" ambition or viewpoint and move more and more into the freedom that Jesus Himself promised as a hundredfold to those who would leave all else: father, mother, wife, husband etc. in order to follow Him (Lk 14:26-27). "If you make My word your home you will indeed be My disciples; you will learn the truth and the truth will make you free" (Jn 8:31-32).

Such freedom is to anticipate even in this life the essential freedom that the saints experience in Heaven. Mary is the model of true human freedom, which consists not primarily in being free to choose between good and evil. This is the lowest kind of freedom that the majority of human beings experience. The freedom that God intended man to possess when He created him according to His image and likeness (Gn 1:26) is the ability on man's part to know, through the Holy Spirit, the *indicative* state of dignity that God's free grace has bestowed on him and then to take his life in his hands and return it totally to God as love given for love received. The *imperative* that St. Paul speaks of so often that must follow upon this realization is the peak of human freedom.

Mary "had" to love God, not through fear, restraint, or an imperative of duty or command of a law. Her whole being recognized that she could not live without God. She freely wished to determine herself at every moment according to God's will and in doing so she knew she was the freest of all human beings. Living consciously toward God, for God, in total virginal surrender brought her at each step to a greater freedom, a greater desire and ability to allow God to be supreme in her life.

VIRGINAL FERTILITY

Mary's virginity was not unto sterility but unto Godly self-giving, loving service. The angel Gabriel did not tell her to go to help her cousin Elizabeth in her pregnancy. Mary, the humble handmaid of the Lord, moved in the oneness she enjoyed with God, pouring out her love in service to all who needed it. Her freedom to determine herself according to her true self, i.e. her whole being centered on God's will, brought her creativity as a loving human being.

She sensitively saw the impending embarrassment of a bride and groom whose wedding party would soon have no more wine and she was free enough to ask and wait on her Son's wish. "They have no wine" . . . "Do whatever He tells you" (Jn 2:4-5).

But her greatest realization came at the foot of the Cross when her virginal surrender reached the peak of her human suffering in total gift to be used by God for His purposes. And her Son gave her to serve the Church: "Woman, this is your son" (Jn 19:26). From that moment, leading to Pentecost and the remaining years of her earthly life, including the 2,000 years of the formation of the Body of her Son the Church, Mary's virginity has blossomed forth into rich harvests. Because she brought forth her only Son and freely strove to be a sign of God's greatness in self-giving by total virginity, Mary has been able to bring forth a progeny more numerous than "the grains of sand on the ground" (Gn 13:16) promised to Abraham. "Yes, from this day forward all generations will call me blessed, for the Almighty has done great things for me" (Lk 1:48).

Mary the Virgin is the promise of what humanity can be. The freedom she enjoyed and still enjoys in her glorified presence to God, her Lord and Savior, is what we are all called to grow into progressively throughout our whole life on earth and in the life to come. Virginity is a process of experiencing God's outpouring free love and returning it with a growing surrender of ourselves to God. But the exciting feature about Mary's virginity and ours is that it is always a state in process of becoming more the virgin-spouse of God. It never reaches a static point of being now complete virginity. As we experience God's free and total gift of Himself to us, we are more emptied of self to be free to serve God and thus bring His life into greater reality for this world. That is why Mary Virgin becomes Mary the Mother of God.

I SING MARY

I sing Mary in the morning
every morning of the year,
because Mary was the dawning
for the Christ-Day to appear,
O yes Mary was the dawning
for the Christ-Day to appear.

I sing Mary in the evening
every evening, every night,

because Mary was the evening
through which the Christ-Star shed his light,
O yes Mary was the evening
through which the Christ-Star shed his light.

So I sing Mary, virgin Mary,
mother Mary, time and time again,
because Mary was the evening
through which the Christ-Star shed his light.

I sing Mary every hour
every hour that I can,
because Mary was the flour
for the Christ-Bread made for man,
O yes Mary was the flour
for the Christ-Bread made for man.

I sing Mary every season
summer, winter, spring and fall,
because Mary was the season
through which the Christ-Life lives in all,
O yes Mary was the season
through which the Christ-Life lives in all.

So I sing Mary, virgin Mary,
mother Mary, time and time again
because Mary was the season
through which the Christ-Life lives in all.

                                        Bill Peffley

3

Mary — Mother of God

Christians have always called Mary the Mother of God and this throughout 2,000 years of reflecting upon Holy Scripture as informed by apostolic tradition. The basis for her greatness and our tender love for her is that she freely cooperated to answer "yes" to the Almighty God, the Heavenly Father and Source of all life, who asked her to give herself as virginal earth so that the Divine Seed, His Word, might become enfleshed.

When the third ecumenical Council of Ephesus (431) fought bitterly the teaching of Nestorius who insisted that Mary was merely the mother of Christ, the man of Nazareth but not in any way the mother of God, the Church realized that the whole of Christianity was at stake. The mystery of Jesus Christ, the union of the completely perfect divinity and humanity, meant for the Councils of Ephesus and Chalcedon (451) that both natures were distinct, though not separated, unmixed, indivisible. Mary, the Church knew, gave birth to a person. This person existed from all eternity, "Light from Light, true God from true God, begotten not made, of one substance with the Father..." as the Nicene Creed (325) expressed the

pre-existent Word. It was this Word that fashioned through
the power of the Holy Spirit a human nature from Mary
virgin.

St. John Damascene, the last in the line of Greek
Fathers, insists that the Son of God, the subsisting "Power
of the Most High," who overshadows the Holy Virgin,
forms a body for Himself. The coming of the Word preceded the formation of the body.

> The angel did not say that the conception should take place
> first and then the indwelling of God, but that the conception
> should be accomplished through the coming and the operation
> of the Holy Spirit and by the indwelling of the Word of God,
> so that the overshadowing of the Power of the Most High
> should take place first, that is, the conception of the Word and
> then the existence of the flesh subsisting in the Word.[1]

A FREE CONSENT

But Mary was not a mere physical "container" to
contain the Uncontainable. She was asked by God, as St.
Luke in his first chapter describes God's message brought
to Mary through the angel, to accept God's request that
she allow Him to work His love in her life totally as He
would wish to do so. It is in Mary's free consent to obey
God by a total surrender in faith that she becomes great by
becoming the mother of the Son of God. By freely surrendering herself to God's will, Mary bound herself in the
most perfect human act of highest freedom to cooperate in
God's saving plan to divinize mankind. By Mary's continued "yes" to God before and after the Incarnation, she
continued to exercise her role as mothering all human beings into the Christic race of children of God. Mary's

motherhood of God cannot be viewed in static terms of a physical mother but must be seen as a consequence of her self-surrender as the handmaid of God's Word. She receives God's objective redemption as full of grace, God's life, and becomes subjectively redeemed and sanctified as the virgin, the surrendering servant, that becomes the mother of God and the mother of all reborn by His Spirit.

GOD'S KENOTIC LOVE

St. Paul had grasped the essence of God's self-giving love as a *kenosis,* an emptying. That Greek word contains a great mystery for us. God's outpouring did not begin only on the Cross when He, whose state was divine, did not cling "to His equality with God but emptied Himself to assume the condition of a slave. . .even to accepting death, death on a cross. . ." (Ph 2:6-8). God's kenosis began when He freely poured Himself out in a multitude of wonderful creatures whom He created "good." Man and woman were to harmonize this richness, constantly experiencing God's outpouring love as they used each creature. Man communicated with God through the intellect and will God had implanted in him. The Book of Genesis describes in mythic language how man turned away from God. He no longer believed in God's emptying love. He sought his autonomous independence. He would take the gifts but refuse to see them as a part of God's emptying love for man.

God had planned the whole world to be united in His own Divine Life, but man turned away from the plan of God. Through sin the world is groaning in disharmony. As St. Maximus the Confessor expressed it:

All existence is splintered into antipodes of the created world
and the uncreated God, the sensible and the intelligible, earth
and heaven, the world and Paradise, masculine and feminine.
Instead of diversity in unity as willed by God, the cosmic reality of death that so graphically separates man's soul from his
body reigns over the universe, separating and dividing what
was meant to be united.[2]

St. Paul describes the world of man's "bondage to
sin" as being caught in the "sarx" (flesh) state. It is man
and his world in all their creaturehood in contrast to God.
It is man, not only in his distance and difference from
God, in his mortality and weakness, but also in his utter estrangement from God through sin. "All have sinned and
lack the approval of God"(Rm 3:23). Again Paul describes
man's existential situation: "Sin entered the world through
one man, and through sin, death, and thus death has
spread through the whole human race because everyone
has sinned" (Rm 5:12). But God so loved this world that
He gave it His only begotten Son (Jn 3:16). Into this
world, groaning in travail, God sent His Son. Although personally sinless, Christ came "in the likeness of sinful
flesh" (Rm 8:3). For our sakes "God made sin of Him
who knew no sin, so that in Him we might become God's
holiness" (2 Co 5:21). Christ took upon Himself this same
estrangement. Although united intimately with the Father,
Christ in His earthly existence was in some sense not fully
one with His Father. He who was infinite "localized" Himself within the humanity that Mary His mother fashioned
for Him.

God's infinite love and mercy condescends *(synkatabasis)* to insert itself within the human race. God made
good that which man in the darkness of his sinful misery

could not accomplish (Rm 15:8-9; 11:32; 5:8). St. Irenaeus in the second century develops the role of Jesus Christ and also Mary in union with Him as one of *anakephalaiosis,* a recapitulation, an undoing of the work of Adam and Eve, a fulfillment going even beyond that originally planned by God if man had never sinned. He writes simply that the end of the Incarnation and redemptive process is: God became man in order that man might become God.

> Christ has, therefore, in His work of recapitulation, summed up all things, both waging war against our enemy and crushing him who at the beginning had led us away captive in Adam. . . in order that, as our species went down to death through a vanquished man, so we may ascend to life through a victorious one.[3]

The process of God's mercy becoming incarnated in Jesus Christ to lead us back has been most clearly and powerfully portrayed by that pillar of orthodoxy in the early Church: St. Athanasius. Defending the full divinity of Jesus Christ against the Arians, Athanasius highlights the condescending mercy of God in Christ Jesus who comes down to us *(synkatabasis)* in order to share with us His divine sonship.

> The Son of God became the Son of man in order that the sons of men, the sons of Adam, might be made sons of God. The Word, who was begotten of the Father in Heaven in an ineffable, inexplicable, incomprehensible and eternal manner, came to this earth to be born in time of the Virgin Mary, Mother of God, in order that they who were born of earth might be born again of God in Heaven. . .He has bestowed upon us the first fruits of the Holy Spirit, so that we may all become sons of God in imitation of the Son of God. Thus He, the true and natural Son of God, bears us all in Himself, so that we may all bear in ourselves the only God.[4]

The Incarnation is the acting out in human, concrete form of God's infinite mercy. His *Hesed* Covenant is no longer posited on His word of fidelity spoken to His Chosen People through His Prophets. Now God's very own Word leapt out of the Trinity and "pitched His tent among us" (Jn 1:14). He emptied Himself of His *Shekinah* (glory) and became an empty receptacle to be filled at each moment of His human growth with the loving mercy of His Father. He takes upon Himself our state of estrangement from the Father.

The condescending mercy of God adapts itself to man's condition. "When the appointed time came, God sent His Son, born of a woman, born a subject of the Law, to redeem the subjects of the Law and to enable us to be adopted as sons" (Ga 4:4-5). Now in human language, especially the language of love that speaks the loudest and clearest, suffering unto death, God's love would be spoken for each person who would care to hear this Word of love. God's plan to heal man's loneliness is to give him His only Begotten Son, Jesus Christ, to act out in terms of human suffering, the infinite love of the Father. We have now no other way of knowing the Father but through His Word made flesh.

The *kenosis* of God's merciful love for us reaches its peak of emptying in the total giving of Jesus to us on the Cross. Seeing God pour Himself out completely, "obedient unto death, the death of the cross" (Ph 2:8), we can believe in God's fidelity toward us in all our needs. God truly is love (1 Jn 4:8; 16). We can believe that God has pursued our adulterous hearts like Hosea and still He espouses us as His Bride: the Church. "That is why I am going to lure her and lead her out into the wilderness and speak to her heart. . . .I will betroth you to myself forever, betroth you with integrity and justice, with tenderness and love" (Ho 2:16; 21).

GOD IN SEARCH OF A MOTHER

Recently there has been much discussion, precipitated by the women's liberation movement, as to whether our theological understanding of God has not been too masculine to the detriment of the feminine. For our purpose here it can be said that Fatherhood, as Louis Bouyer has pointed out, belongs to God alone in His essence of absolute Source of Being.[5] Only God is totally perfect, complete, independent and therefore He alone is *Love,* capable of sharing Himself in free gift. It is of the essence of creatures not to be their own source of being, but to be utterly dependent upon God as their Source. Even when a human being becomes a father, it is not of his essence to be always a father. But it is of the essence of human creatures to be dependent and therefore to be virginal in their barrenness and poverty. Their whole being cries out in complete potentiality to be fulfilled by another. Motherhood is receiving life from another and bringing this forth into a new creature. It is more in keeping with our human creatureliness to see motherhood as belonging to us, not to God.

The first woman, Eve, as the Greek Fathers constantly recall, was virgin that refused to be the dependent mother as God wished her to be. She refused to accept her dependence upon the Fatherhood of God. She was tempted: "You shall be like gods, knowing good and evil" (Gn 3:5). Sin is denying the Fatherhood of God, that all things come to us as gifts from His free, merciful love. It is refusing also to recognize the virginal-motherhood that is basic barrenness before God, crying out to receive His gifts of life and love.

God sought out the New Woman, Mary, to begin again a new creation. God would "recapitulate" His creation beginning with a woman who would freely consent to do what Eve refused to do: to be total woman, virgin and mother. She would be the climax of the *Anawim,* the Remnant of God, where God would slowly evolve His new people into the perfect archetype of the future Church. Mary is the fulfilled humanity in microcosmic fashion, that which the whole of humanity must eventually become by God's Holy Spirit: the woman who is total dependence, absolute potential before God. She renounces her autonomy and accepts to be the poor servant of God. In this is Mary's greatness and the greatness of every other human being.

A PATRISTIC VIEW OF MARY – NEW EVE

In Christian devotion to Mary there has always been a danger of making her divine motherhood a mere physical endowment instead of placing Mary and her self-determination to cooperate with Jesus Christ, the New Adam, into the whole drama of the history of salvation. By returning to the early Fathers of the Church and developing their concept of Mary as New Eve we can avoid such an error. She will not be a fourth member vying for divinity, but she will be the epitome of all that God has decreed mankind to be through cooperation with grace. Only by keeping in mind what Mary's *fiat* meant in the whole picture of God's merciful condescension to redeem us through Jesus Christ can we truly understand her divine motherhood and also prepare ourselves for a proper veneration of her as our mother and the model of the Universal Church.

The apologetic writer and martyr, Justin (+c. 165), is the first Father to employ this analogy of Mary as the New Eve. In his *Dialogue with Trypho,* after a long involved development of Isaiah 7:14, Justin makes his comparison:

> Christ became man through the Virgin in order that disobedience which issued from the serpent might be destroyed in the same way in which it took its origin. In fact Eve was still an incorrupt virgin when she conceived in her womb the word which came to her from the serpent and she brought forth disobedience and death. On the contrary, it is in faith and joy that Mary the Virgin conceives when the Angel Gabriel announces to her. . .to which news she answers: 'May it be done unto me according to your word.' Thus through the intermediation of this Virgin He came into the world. . .through whom God would crush the serpent and others similar to him, angels and men, and who delivers from death those who return from their evil sentiments and believe in Him.[6]

Here we see an analogy between Mary and Eve in its primitive state: a parallelism in God's designs of effecting man's redemption in a similar way as man's spiritual destruction and death were brought about. Both are virgins who then give birth, one through disobedience to death while the other through faith and joy to Him who is the salvation of the human race. There is no attempt on his part to analyze in profundity the role of Mary in cooperating with the regeneration of men.

RECAPITULATION

Irenaeus (+202) treats of this analogy in great detail and can be considered the first Marian theologian. The analogy that he uses of Mary as the New Eve is intimately connected with his fundamental theological principle of recapitulation.[7] In the setting of Christ, as the new head restoring the human race to its former state of divine friendship, Mary takes her place in this process of restoration.

> Just as Eve, wife of Adam, yes, yet still a virgin. . .became by her disobedience the cause of death for herself and the whole human race, so Mary, too, espoused, yet a virgin, became by her obedience the cause of salvation for herself and the whole human race. And this is why the Law calls her who was espoused to a man the wife of him who had espoused her, though she was still a virgin: to show the cycle that goes back *(recirculationem)* from Mary to Eve. The point is, what is tied together cannot possibly be untied save by inversion of the process whereby the bonds of union have arisen, so that the original ties are loosed by the subsequent, and the subsequent set the original free. . .and so it was that the knot of Eve's disobedience was loosed by Mary's obedience. For what the virgin Eve bound fast by her refusal to believe, this the Virgin Mary unbound by her belief.[8]

The *recirculatio* envisioned in this analogy by Irenaeus ties Mary intimately with the recapitulation by Christ of the human race and boldly reproduces in each detail the whole process, but now in reverse. The accent is placed on the antithesis between the first Eve and the New Eve. Both are virgins, one disobedient, the other obedient. We see easily here the same text quoted before from Justin. But for Irenaeus the analogy does not remain only a similitude of externals. Mary as Mother of the Savior has an active part in "untying" the knot of original sin. This is more closely seen in another text of Irenaeus written after the above text.

Christ recapitulated by the obedience on a tree (cross) the disobedience that took place on a tree; and, to the destruction of
that seduction whereby the betrothed virgin Eve was evilly
seduced, the glad tidings of truth were happily brought by an
angel to Mary, virgin espoused. For, as Eve was seduced by the
utterance of an angel to flee God after disobeying His word, so
Mary by the utterance of an angel had the glad tidings brought
to her, that she should bear God in obedience to His word.
And whereas Eve had disobeyed God, Mary was persuaded to
obey God, that the Virgin Mary might become intercessor
(advocata) of the virgin Eve. And as the human race was sen-
tenced to death by means of a virgin, by means of a virgin is it
delivered *(salvatur)*. A virgin's disobedience is balanced by a
virgin's obedience. For the sin of the first-formed was emend-
ed by the correction from the First-born; the guilt of the serpent was overcome by the simplicity of the dove; and we were
set free from those chains by which we had been bound to
death.[9]

In all these inter-related texts of Irenaeus we find a
common theme: it is through the Incarnation that Jesus
Christ becomes the "recapitulator," assuming in Himself
all of humanity and restoring all things through the Incarnation back to their pristine orientation to the glory of
God and to the attainment of their own fullest perfection.
Mary overcomes the disobedience of Eve and hence the
evil effects caused by her original sin, death, meaning primarily, in the eschatological sense, supernatural death in
the soul through loss of God's life and final damnation;
she does this by pronouncing her freely given "fiat." Thus
she becomes the mother of the human race through estab-
lishing them again in the spiritual life; in this she is insepar-
ably united to the New Adam.

Irenaeus does not enter into the causality exerted by

the Virgin in the redemption of the human race but simply is content to use the word *"salvatur."* For him and for the other early Fathers it would have no meaning to ask what causality she exerted in the redemption, for this was a co-operation between God and a human being, a *synergeia* that could not be divided into quantitative parts. The value of Irenaeus' texts for us lies precisely in the fact that he did not formulate conclusions in terms of our contemporary Marian theology, i.e. co-redemption, co-mediation, etc. In not doing thusly, he kept the dynamism of the analogy of Mary and the Church one of identity and unity. Thus the role of Mary in the redemption is one situated close to the Redeemer which can never be considered aside from her intimate relationship to Him.

No Father, either of the East or the West, developed this theme of Eve-Mary so well as did St. Epiphanius (+403). He was born and educated in Palestine and thus can be considered in the Syrian-Palestinian line of Irenaeus as opposed to the Alexandrian-Cappadocian line that did not develop this theme. In his *Panarion* he devotes two chapters to draw out of this parallel the most advanced Marian theology of his time. Here we see type and anti-type of the Oriental mind applied to Mary in a mentality that is consistent with the same biblical mind that provides us with a link between the Old Testament and the New by seeing the overall plan of God in the continual history of salvation.

It is she (Mary) who was intended through Eve. Eve it was who received in figure the name of Mother of the living. For Eve had been called this after she had heard the words 'You are dust and unto dust you shall return.' It was an amazing thing that after she had sinned she should receive this magnificent name. We must not see only the sensible reality that from her the whole human race on earth would take its birth but according to the truth that it is Mary from whom life itself would be born for the world because it was she who gave birth to a life and thus Mary became mother of the living. It is then in figure that Mary has been called Mother of the living.[10]

MARY – MOTHER OF LIFE

We see here the Platonic as well as the Johannine language coupled with the biblical language and prophecies of the Old Testament linked with the new alliance. Eve's physical maternity is only a figure anticipating the only real maternity whereby Mary would give birth to Life, and through this Life, Christ, the whole human race would be reborn again in God's life. Mary is thus the true Mother of the living and this is said of Eve only as a figure to be fulfilled more perfectly in Mary.

St. Epiphanius goes on to develop St. John's concept of Life linking it with the New Man of St. Paul.

But we must still consider another marvelous thing in regard to the subject of Eve and Mary. Eve had been for men an occasion of death and through her, death entered into the world. Mary had been the occasion of life and through her, life had been born in us. It is for this reason that the Son of God has come into the world. 'There where sin had abounded, grace had more abounded' (Rm 5:20). . . .When death came, life came and more of it in order that life might come in place of death, chasing death which came to us through a woman. And He came to us precisely through a woman and thus became for us the life. Since Eve, still a virgin, had sin through her disobedience, obedience of grace came through also a virgin when it was announced to her that God, Life

eternal, would descend from heaven and be born in flesh. . . .
All this cannot be accomplished absolutely in her (Eve), but it
is accomplished in truth in this Seed, holy and chosen absolutely unique which came from Mary and not from any union
with man. It is He who came to destroy the power of the
dragon, of the twisting, fleeing serpent. . .This is why the Only
Begotten came from a woman, to destroy the serpent, that is
today, the wicked doctrine, corruptor of life, error and in-
iquity.[11]

Thus, in linking up death to Eve and life to Mary,
Epiphanius ties up very well this parallel of Eve-Mary to
Adam-Christ found in Paul's epistles, especially that to
Romans. As Adam had been the cause of death (not just
physical death) to the human race, and Christ was the
cause of life through His free oblation of self to His Father
in obedience to the "death of the Cross," so Eve had been
the cause of the loss of divine life in us in her intimate association with Adam in the one act of sin while Mary has
been the source of the restoration of divine life in us in her
intimate association with Christ in His one act of redemption of the human race.

A DYNAMIC PARALLELISM

This cursory presentation of the Fathers' understanding of Mary as the Mother of God and our Mother has been
centered around the parallel between Eve and Mary. It
cannot be seen as a mere analogy or a static comparison.
The parallel is usually represented as a part of the recapitulation by Christ of the whole human race back to the original man, made to God's image and likeness. Often we find
an exact correspondence of details, two virgins, two ma-
ternities, temptation by the serpent and the joyful an-

nouncement by the archangel, the disobedience of Eve and the free act of obedience of Mary, restoring life for death, not only eschatologically in the glorified state of immortality but more proximately in the present state of divine life in the souls of men through grace. Behind all these details of parallelism there is the fundamental idea of a re-beginning, of a return to a former state.

But, as has been stated earlier, unless we can think in the perspective of the early Fathers, in their fourth dimension of seeing the entire design of God in a full sweep of salvific history embracing each and every moment of God's merciful dealings with mankind, we will look upon this as a mere literary device of convenience. Through this image, Eve is a figure, a type of Mary as the first shadowing, imperfect, preparatory for a more nuptial union between God and humanity to be realized in Mary first and then in the Church. The two elements of the first Eve that were restored to their primitive perfection by the second Eve and were to be carried out by the third Eve, the Church, are *virginity* and the *"mother of the Living."*

Virginity among the Fathers means more than mere physical integrity. It refers more to the mystical union of individual souls with God in an habitual attitude of loving submission to God's holy will. Thus we find the element of Eve's disobedience the source of death and enmity with God while Mary's obedience is the source of life and most intimate union summarized by the words of Genesis: "And they shall be two in one body." In this respect Mary's co-operation in the redemption of the human race is one of intimate union as *socia* or companion used by God, not only in order that God could penetrate into the temporal, the human, the finite, but also that Mary might remain the perfect example for the Church as *Socia* to Christ in cooperating with the Second Adam, the New Man, Christ, in restoring the whole created world and in transfiguring it into that which perfectly mirrors forth God's plan from all eternity.

Mary, as the first Eve, is mother of men, but of living men, living with the life of God in their souls. Here the analogy between the first Eve and the second falls down insofar as Mary is not the transmitter of new life through a spouse relationship toward Christ. Her spiritual maternity toward the newly born in Baptism flows from her relationship to Christ as Mother to Son. Thus in the area of maternity, the three Eves, Eve-Mary-Church, are analogically mothers, in different ways and degrees. Epiphanius, as we have seen, best brings out the motherhood of Mary. She is the mother of the spiritual living by bringing *Life* into the world, Jesus Christ, her only begotten son.

The Fathers imply, because her maternity was not purely passive but an active receptivity of Divine Life in her womb through her faith and obedience, that she exerted an active role in the redemption of the human race. But no Father has developed fully all the implications. This would be left for later centuries, to see in the seeds of this relationship of Mary to the first Eve the basis of a true Marian theology and devotion. The most important feature, I believe, is that they bequeathed to us the principle of recapitulation and recirculation, Mary with the New Adam, in bringing new life to individuals in whom death had come through the first Adam. By keeping Mary's role intimately united with that of Christ as His *socia* through her free act of faith and obedience, her virginity of total dedication to God's divine plan of redemption, we will be better able to understand how Mary is truly the mother of the living, of the People of God.

MARY – THEOTOKOS

It was at the Council of Ephesus (431), as has already been stated, that the whole consistent patristic doctrine of Mary as Begetter of Divine Life converged around the battlecry of *Theotokos,* in Greek, the Birth-Giver of God. As long as Christians were rooted in Scripture and the patristic tradition that stressed Mary's total surrender in obedient faith, there was the solid basis for a true devotion to Mary. And we are also enabled to keep in clear focus the graceful dignity to which we have all been called because Mary consented to say "yes" to God's proposal that she offer motherhood in order that the Holy Trinity could break into our world of potential and allow His *agape* to be brought into full fruition, filling us with "the utter fulness of God" (Ep 3:19).

Because she was total virgin-mother to God, we can greet her along with Elizabeth as the mother of our Lord (Lk 1:43). We can profess with joy that what is born of her "will be called Son of God" (Lk 1:35). With Mary we can praise God, proclaiming His greatness "because He has looked upon His lowly handmaid" (Lk 1:46-47). Yes, Mary, Mother of God, all generations will call you blessed for the Almighty has done great things for you. He has exalted the lowly servant of God and made you His Mother (Lk 1:48, 52).

TITLES OF MARY

Mary has said *yes* for the whole human race. God is love and He wishes to pour His very own life into us. Mary is the sign of what we all can become by grace. She is the *Gate of Heaven* through which we are saved. She freely gave her consent; yet her freedom to do so was totally graced by God's free choice and the sending of His Holy Spirit upon her. Because, as St. Bernard says of her, she only sought God's grace, she always was "full of grace." She understood, as none of us has, that all is God's grace and she is nothing but God's desire in her to receive His love.

Mary is the point of humanity where there converges through grace of God the holiness of human perfection that consists in a continued hunger and thirst for greater union with God. This is what ultimately her motherhood means. It is not merely relegated to the one static moment when she brought forth, as mother, Jesus Christ, the Son of God. She is progressively always becoming the mother of God just as the Church and we members of the Church are called out to become also like Mary, the begetter of the Son of God through our continued desire for union through loving submission to God's holy will.

Because Mary concretizes what lies deeply within all of us in potential, namely, to be oriented to Christ as a mother begets new life since we have been made "according to the image and likeness" (Gn 1:26) that is Jesus Christ, we can resonate with various titles that Christian piety throughout the centuries have formulated to express this archetypal symbol of Mary as mother, the great mother of God.

Many such titles deal with earth symbolism. John Damascene calls Mary "the unploughed field," "the unwatered vineyard."[12] St. Ephrem eulogizes her as "God's Eden."[13] St. Theodotus names her "earth unsown that flowered forth fruit that saves."[14]

The uroboric (great mother) characteristic of protection, nourishment, preserver is maintained throughout Christian devotion in addressing Mary as mother. Such symbols are in terms of the vessel, the pot, the dwelling, house, cave or temple, which refer to enclosures that encompass to protect, nourish and provide rest. One of the great archetypal mother-images used in the Christian East, Mary as temple of God, developed into one of the great feasts in the East to Mary, Mother of God, i.e. her Presentation in the Temple (Nov. 21). For the pragmatic Western Christian, such a feast is seen as solely an unhistorical detail taken from apocryphal writings that sprang up in the third and fourth centuries to feed the piety of the unlearned masses of Christians who were curious about the areas of the life of Mary not developed or mentioned in the Gospel.

MARY – GOD'S TEMPLE

On this simple feast the faithful commemorate Mary as replacing the Old Temple and becoming the New Temple of God. She becomes the archetype of all Christians as St. Paul exhorted the Corinthians: "Didn't you realize that you were God's temple and that the Spirit of God was living among you? If anybody should destroy the temple of God, God will destroy him because the temple of God is sacred and you are that temple" (1 Co 3:16-17). Mary is brought into God's temple and becomes God's temple. With her the whole of humanity, the Church, becomes the focal point, the enclosure where God consents to be "present" in His loving, divinizing presence. Her dedication at the early age of three to God's service is the Church contemplating Mary's complete virginal-motherhood from the first moments of her consciousness of who God is for her and who she is in response to Him.

In most Greek Byzantine churches, Mary is depicted in fresco or mosaic in the apse behind the altar, on high. She is called the "Platytera," the broader-than-the-heavens. She is shown stretching out her arms in a protective posture of a loving mother, a protective hen, a temple containing the uncontainable. When we fail to move in prayer and devotion to a level beyond black and white concepts, to enter into the sacred world of archetypal symbols, we shall also fail to understand Mary as our Great Mother and our Christian call also to be mother to the Word of God.

Yet such mother-symbols of nourishment and protection are part of Christian devotion to Mary as mother of Christ and our mother too. St. Germanus of Constantinople (+720), for example, calls Mary, "wholly the dwelling place of God."[15] St. Ephrem the Syrian (+373) says she is the "dwelling and habitation of the Spirit."[16] St. Cyril of Alexandria describes her as "the indestructible temple, the dwelling of the Illimitable."[17] The beautiful, favorite prayer to Mary in the Byzantine Church, the *Akathistos,* sings of Mary as: "Hail! tabernacle of God and the Word! Hail! ark gilded by the Holy Spirit."[18] St. Jerome calls her, "the temple of the Lord's body," "the sanctuary of the Holy Spirit."[19] In the Byzantine Liturgy, on the vigil of Our Lady's Presentation, Mary is called "the true temple of the Divine Word."[20]

Christian piety has constantly venerated Mary as the physical mother of God. Also, because she is spiritual and totally committed to serve God with joyful abandonment, as mother she can be seen in a spousal relationship with Jesus Christ. It is this that enforces our ability to call Mary, Mother Church. Mary becomes the eternal Spouse of

Jesus Christ through the archetypal symbols of mother-son love myths where the basic idea is that of transformation of the mother by the offspring. Here we see the many symbols that describe Mary and Christ as Dawn and Sun. "O Spendid Dawn, that has brought us the Sun who is Christ" is a continued epithet addressed to Mary. Her Son, the Sun of the darkened world, is heralded by the Dawn, Mary. Yet the Dawn receives all its light from the Sun that has not yet appeared. Mary is immaculately conceived by Jesus Christ in anticipation of her heralding His coming. He transfigures her, making her a sharer in His nature in order that she might give Him her human nature.

Mary as Mother of God will always be for Christians, led by the Holy Spirit to understand the greatness of Jesus Christ, their favorite title addressed to her, for it invokes the poverty of the handmaid of God as empty virgin receiving God's infinite love into her consciousness, her "heart." It suggests her total "yes" in a growing process of responding to God's plans. It suggests a potency called by her active response in grace to be actualized as truly the mother who gives birth to the Son of God.

Above all, as we Christians stand before her icons or statues, praying the Rosary at her shrines or kneeling at our bedside, the Spirit of God opens up to us the vision of the beloved disciple, John, who took her to himself as his mother: "Now a great sign appeared in Heaven: a woman, adorned with the sun, standing on the moon, and with the twelve stars on her head for a crown" (Rv 12:1). By God's grace we realize the gift Mary is as our loving Mother and in muted voices of reverence and surrendering love we echo back to her: "Holy Mary, Mother of God, pray for us sinners now and at the hour of our death. Amen."

A MOTHER AND A LITTLE CHILD

A mother and a little child
came into the world and smiled
earth has never been the same
since they came
with their touch of spring
men called Him little king
and her his undefiled. . .
the Mother and the little Child.

A mother and a growing boy
brought the world a special joy
sharing all our common ways
nights and days
as a family,
none knew their destiny
earth could have been his toy. . .
the Mother and the growing Boy.

A mother and a dying son
loved the world with hearts as one
through His death on Calvary
in you and me
He has come to dwell
earth cries "Emmanuel,
see what their love has done!". . .
the Mother and the dying Son.

Bill Peffley

4

Mary and the Holy Spirit

The Holy Spirit cannot be pictured; He must be experienced. But because He is the presence of God's glory, His *Shekinah,* He is experienced as a fulfilling richness. He is present and filling where there is a void and emptiness. He is present and bringing light where darkness cries out for healing.

We find the Holy Spirit in *Genesis* hovering like a cosmic bird over the earth, seeking to stir the cosmos out of its slumbering impotence to fullness of life. "The Spirit of the Lord brooded over the waters" (Gn 1:2). In the Book of Deuteronomy the Spirit of God is pictured as an eagle hovering over its brood. "Like an eagle watching its nest, hovering over its young, He spreads out His wings to hold him; He supports him on His pinions" (Dt 32:11). Not only is the Spirit eager to protect God's chosen children by His overarching, loving protection, but He can be seen in this biblical picture as a force that stirs life to greater life.

This eagle image for the Israelites of the desert was very rich with meaning. Often they had seen the mother eagle take the individual eaglet on its strong pinions and fly up into the sky. At a given moment, the mother eagle would dip from under the eaglet, leaving the little eagle alone in mid-air to fly upward or to plummet downward. The eagle would quickly fly under the falling eaglet to catch it again, to bear it up on its pinions only to repeat the process until the eaglet let go of fear and soared up into the heavens – an eagle at last!

The Holy Spirit is the *Ruah,* the wind and the breath that blow over the universe creating a loving relationship between God and man. That very breath of God is breathed into man's nostrils, "Then He breathed into his nostrils a breath of life, and thus man became a living being" (Gn 2:7).

"THE HOLY SPIRIT WILL COME UPON YOU"

God's protective Spirit hovered like a cloud over the Israelites in the desert. He came upon Saul, the anointed king. He was the power in Samson and David, the prophetic voice in the prophets Isaiah and Jeremiah. God's Spirit was always creating new hearts (Ps 51:10) in men of good will. No man, created according to God's image and likeness (Gn 1:26), could ever escape from God's Spirit, His loving, active presence (Ps 139:7).

Yet in a dry and barren desert called earth, God's Holy Spirit hovered over an oasis, fresh with God's life. Mary was that "place" over which God's protective cloud hovered from her first moment of existence. Her *Immaculate Conception,* declared a dogma in 1854 by Pope Pius IX, is the Church's celebration of God's Love, the Holy Spirit, coming over Mary at the first moment of conception and giving her a continued growth in awareness that her whole being was a temple of God and the Holy Spirit dwelt within her in a very special way (1 Co 3:16).

Mary's greatness consists in her cooperation with the Holy Spirit. She is the model of all Christians precisely because she yielded always to the power of the Holy Spirit that continually came upon her. She is truly the charismatic Christian, par excellence, because she cooperated at every moment of her conscious life in faith and obedience with the movements of the Holy Spirit.

MESSIANIC GENEALOGY

St. Matthew's account of Mary's conception of Jesus through the Holy Spirit (Mt 1:18) is tied with his genealogy which opens his Gospel (Mt 1:1-17). He highlights, by tracing Jesus' lineage through the recipients of the messianic promises, especially Abraham and David, the new beginning, a new genesis for humanity in the virginal conception by the creative action of the Holy Spirit. In the Yahwistic account of the creation of the first man (Gn 2:7), God breathes into man His spirit.

Now in Matthew's account, it is the same Spirit breathing into the Virgin Mary Divine Life, and the New Man, Christ, is conceived. Jesus is the beginning of the new Genesis, the new Adam, the father of the messianic people of God. Abraham and David were the messianic forerunners who were types of a new nation more numerous than the sands of the seashore. Jesus comes as the completion, but even before Abraham, He existed. He becomes man through the cooperation of Mary and the Holy Spirit. The *Qahal,* the assembly of God's chosen people, begins with the Spirit breathing into Abraham and David and the forerunners of Christ a faith that would expect the prophecy of a new race to come from the Spirit and a virgin.

St. Matthew is noted for his linking up of the Old Testament prophecies with their fulfillment in the New Covenant. Not only does he explicitly call attention to the prophecy of Isaiah 7:14: "The virgin will conceive and give birth to a son and they will call him Emmanuel" which would be brought about by the Holy Spirit (Mt 1:20), but he also implicitly recalls our attention to the prophecy of Genesis 3:15:

> I will make you enemies of each other: you and the woman, your offspring and her offspring. It will crush your head and you will strike its heel.

The woman of Genesis and the virgin of Isaiah is Mary. "She will give birth to a son and you must name Him Jesus, because He is the one who is to save His people from their sins" (Mt 1:21). The coming of the Messiah from a woman is to be effected by the Holy Spirit. But His birth is also tied to the birth of the messianic people of God. The Church is being shaped at the Annunciation. The Messiah and the Church are "born of the Spirit." Mary is already seen as the New Eve, the Mother of the new people of God.

ST. LUKE'S GENEALOGY

The relationship of Mary and the Holy Spirit in regard to the virginal birth of Christ and the birth of the people of God is highlighted even more strongly by St. Luke.

Lucien Cerfaux points out that Luke's Gospel and the

Acts of the Apostles form one whole.[1] The Angel Gabriel announces to Mary: "The Holy Spirit will come upon you" (Lk 1:35). To understand St. Luke's teaching of Mary and the Holy Spirit, we must see the full meaning of that phrase: "will come upon," (*eperchesthai* in Greek).

The prophet Isaiah had foretold: "Once more there will be poured on us the Spirit from above; then shall the wilderness be fertile land and fertile land become forest" (Is 32:15).

The prophet Ezekiel also sees a new beginning, an eschatological restoration from sterility to fertility that gives St. Luke another source for his phrase:

> I shall pour clean water over you and you will be cleansed; I shall cleanse you of all your defilement and all your idols. I shall give you a new heart, and put a new spirit in you; I shall remove the heart of stone from your bodies and give you a heart of flesh instead. I shall put My spirit in you and make you keep My laws and sincerely respect My observances. . . You shall be My people and I will be your God. . .On the day I cleanse you from all your sins, I will repopulate the cities and cause the ruins to be rebuilt. Wasteland, once desolate for every passer-by to see, will now be farmed again. Everyone will say: This land, so recently a waste, is now like a garden of Eden, and the ruined cities once abandoned and levelled to the ground are now strongholds with people living in them. And the nations left round you will know that I, Yahweh, have rebuilt what was destroyed and replanted what was ruined. I, Yahweh, have spoken, and I will do it (Ezk 36:25-36).

Ezekiel again provides Luke with another image of God's Spirit bringing forth new life in his well-known vision of the valley of dry bones.

The Lord Yahweh says this to these bones: I am now going to make the breath enter you, and you will live. I shall put sinews on you, I shall make flesh grow on you, I shall cover you with skin and give you breath, and you will live; and you will learn that I am Yahweh (Ezk 37:5-7).

LUKE'S NEW CREATION

Luke prefaces his account of the new creation by the Holy Spirit coming upon Mary by giving the story of barren Elizabeth, Mary's cousin. The Holy Spirit coming upon Elizabeth and her child John will be the instrument in bringing God's people back in a restoration. "Even from his mother's womb, he will be filled with the Holy Spirit and he will bring back many of the sons of Israel to the Lord their God. . .preparing for the Lord a people fit for Him" (Lk 1:16-18). This reference must have recalled to Luke the intervention of God to remove the sterility of other ancestors of Mary: Rebecca, Rachel, the mother of Samson, and Hannah.

Mary is to become the flowering root of Jesse. Yet Luke points out, more than Matthew, that Mary's relationship to the Holy Spirit is not one of mere passivity but rather one of freely consenting to give herself completely to God's service. Mary asks the angel how it will be possible to conceive as a virgin. Perhaps Luke used the appearance of the angel to Gideon as his model.[2] "Forgive me, my Lord, but if Yahweh is with us, then why is it that all this is happening to us now?" (Jg 6:13). But as in similar announcements of divine intervention to effect new life (as in Gn 17:18; Jg 13; Lk 1; Ex 3:4) Gideon shows a lack of faith.

Mary, however, does not doubt. She merely wishes to know the direction that God's Spirit is to take in her life. The Holy Spirit had led her to an espousal with Joseph. She was a virgin. Was God's plan to be accomplished through normal marital intercourse or was she to continue as she was—a virgin? "But how can this come about, since I am a virgin?" (Lk 1:34).

It is then that Mary hears explicitly what she must have lived by and experienced profoundly in faith all throughout her previous years of cooperating sensitively to the Holy Spirit's inspiration: "The Holy Spirit will come upon you and the power of the Most High will cover you with its shadow" (Lk 1:35).

What ecstasy she must have felt as she surrendered herself body, soul and spirit, completely, to the coming upon her of the Holy Spirit! Mary, in her moment of free consent to be the pure channel, the spotless temple of the Holy Spirit, moved to a new level of consciousness. She realized that the overshadowing of her all her lifetime by God's Spirit of love was truly an indwelling effecting the miracle of all miracles whereby God took flesh within her.

The awesomeness of that moment has been beautifully verbalized in the Byzantine Vespers for the Feast of the Annunciation:

> The Archangel Gabriel was sent
> From Heaven,
> To bring to the Virgin the glad tidings
> Of her conception.
> Coming to Nazareth and marvelling at the miracle,
> He thought within himself:
> How wonderful that He, whom the heavens
> Cannot comprehend,
> Is born of a Virgin;

That He who has Heaven for a throne
And earth for a footstool
Finds place within a Maiden's womb!
That He, upon whom
The six-winged Seraphim
And the many-eyed Cherubim
Cannot gaze,
Deigns to become incarnate of her
By one single word:
But is the *WORD* of God!
Yet, why do I stand by and say not
To the Virgin:
Hail, full of grace, the Lord is with thee
Hail, Virgin purest one;
Hail, maiden bride!
Hail, Mother of life,
Blessed is the fruit of thy womb!

THE INDWELLING OF THE HOLY SPIRIT

What Christian ever experienced as Mary did at that sacred moment of divine impregnation of the Word of God in her womb not only the presence but the deifying activity of the Holy Spirit within? St. Paul could write: "Didn't you realize that you were God's temple and that the Spirit of God was living among you?" (1 Co 3:16). She knew in that moment what St. Paul meant: "Your body, you know, is the temple of the Holy Spirit, who is in you since you received Him from God" (1 Co 6:19).

The great threshold that marks the breakthrough for a dynamic Christian comes when he or she realizes with ever-new awareness that God's sanctifying power, the Holy Spirit, dwells within oneself and not outside. We fix all our attention inwardly upon the Divine Sanctifier. With such a quickening in her spirit, Mary must have pronounced her "yes" to God's Holy Spirit.

She discovers at that moment God's glorious kingdom in her heart. She drinks at the Spirit's living water from which springs eternal life. She is full of grace and the Spirit inundates her, making her a fertile valley.

God dwells in all spiritually alive Christians but always in different degrees. What accounts for the difference? Is it not what Mary illustrates so beautifully in this scene in St. Luke's Gospel in her *fiat*? God abides more in one saint than in another because the Holy Spirit is given more freedom by the individual.

> If anyone loves Me, he will keep My word, and My Father will love him, and We shall come to him and make Our home with him (Jn 14:23).

The Holy Spirit in Mary and in us also is the Vivifier, making us living members of Jesus Christ and holy temples of God. He is the Spirit of adoption that allows us to know that we really are children of God capable of living lives befitting Abba, our Father (Ga 4:5-7; Rm 8:9-16).

THE GIFT OF THE HOLY SPIRIT

Jesus promised that He would ask the Father to send the Spirit upon the disciples. His words were realized in Mary's experience in the Annunciation:

> I shall ask the Father,
> and He will give you another Advocate
> to be with you forever,

that Spirit of truth
whom the world can never
receive
since it neither sees nor knows Him;
but you know Him
because He is with you, He is in you.
. . .But when the Spirit of truth comes
He will lead you to the complete truth,
since He will not be speaking as from Himself
but will say only what He has learnt
     (Jn 14:15-17; 16:13).

As the Holy Spirit comes upon Mary, she is vivified by God's own life more completely. She is given a more complete understanding of her role in the history of salvation. Possessing the Spirit, Mary possesses the very love of God sanctifying her as His dwelling-place. It is in that overshadowing of Mary by the Holy Spirit that Mary receives the strength to live her new commitment as Mother of the Messiah.

A FORESHADOWING OF PENTECOST

We cannot read Luke's account of the Spirit's overshadowing of Mary without at the same time recalling his account of the Holy Spirit's coming upon Mary in the midst of the Apostles. Jesus had promised in words similar to those used by the Angel Gabriel: ". . .but you will receive power when the Holy Spirit comes on you. . ." (Acts 1:8). We note that St. Luke singles Mary out from among the other women who waited with the Apostles for the coming of the Holy Spirit: "All these joined in continuous prayer, together with several women, including

Mary the mother of Jesus and with His brothers" (Acts 1:14).

In both cases where the Holy Spirit overshadows, first Mary alone, and then Mary and the first believers, in the mind of Luke there is the birth of the Body of Christ, the Church. In Nazareth, Mary is the first Christian who through the power of the overshadowing Holy Spirit gives birth to Jesus. In the Upper Room, she is joined by other believers, men and women, all of whom again experience the coming upon them of the Holy Spirit.

THE HOLY SPIRIT COMES UPON ALL CHRISTIANS

From meditating on Luke's parallel usage of the Holy Spirit's coming upon Mary in the Annunciation and upon her and the Apostles and the other women at Pentecost, the Greek Fathers easily moved the parallel to apply equally well to all Christians.

As the Holy Spirit is always the activator of God's Word in the human soul, Origen teaches that the Spirit brings forth Jesus in the Virgin's womb in order that He may equally be born in each Christian by the same Spirit.

> What meaning does it have to say that Jesus has come only in the flesh which He received from Mary if I do not show He has come also in my flesh?[3]

Again Origen insists that this overshadowing, as in Mary's case, is for us as well and we must want it as she did.

> ...and not only in Mary did this birth begin by the overshadowing of the Holy Spirit but in you also, if you are worthy of it, the Word of God is born. Then seek the ability to

seize this overshadowing and when you will have been made
worthy of this overshadowing, there will come to you through
this overshadowing His body born in you.[4]

A CHANNEL OF THE HOLY SPIRIT

Dr. Irene Claremont de Castillejo, in her book
Knowing Woman,[5] has a beautiful chapter entitled: "The
Rainmaker." She tells of a Chinese village that sought rain
from the magicians and sorcerers but their rituals and
incantations were of no avail. Finally the villagers
approached a little old man and begged him to come to
their village and bring them rain. He asked only for a little
hut on the outside of the village. There he sat for three
days and then the rains came.

Rainmakers do not do things. They are a *presence*.
They are bridges between God and men. When their quiet
presence comes upon people, things happen. God begins to
work in marvelous ways because they are little and allow
Him to be God. They know their own poverty and God
pours His riches through them to those around them
because they are perfect channels of His graces.

It is difficult to judge the importance of a rainmaker
for he does nothing. His constant shout of joy is, "For the
Almighty has done great things for me" (Lk 1:49). Mary is
the greatest rainmaker the world has ever seen. In her
earthly life she did not do so much in human terms. But
she was a presence so that wherever she appeared, the Holy
Spirit burst forth in new and exciting ways.

Mary is the ideal charismatic Christian, not only
because the Holy Spirit came upon her, but also because
she mediated the Holy Spirit to others and she continues

to be a presence to all who ask her to come into their lives and make the rain of the Holy Spirit fall abundantly upon thirsty, parched hearts to bring forth much fruit.

We think of the people that entered into a new outpouring of the Holy Spirit through Mary's presence in their lives. It was St. Joseph who of all human beings was closest to Mary. He loved her from the first moment his eyes saw her. His whole being cried out to be near her as any young man is ready to give up all in order to possess himself in the woman he ardently loves. Yet rain can be accompanied by thunder and lightning, and Joseph was torn in two wondering how his espoused virgin, Mary, could be with child. Mary simply waits for the Holy Spirit to enlighten Joseph.

> He had made up his mind to do this (divorce her informally) when the angel of the Lord appeared to him in a dream and said: 'Joseph, son of David, do not be afraid to take Mary home as your wife, because she has conceived what is in her by the Holy Spirit. She will give birth to a son and you must name Him Jesus, because He is the one who is to save His people from their sins (Mt 1:20-21).

ELIZABETH FILLED WITH THE HOLY SPIRIT

Mary, filled with the Holy Spirit is impelled out of love to rush to the aid of her cousin, Elizabeth, in her pregnancy. And there Mary's presence brings the Holy Spirit both to Elizabeth and to her child in her womb, John the Baptist. As soon as Elizabeth heard Mary's simple presence, the power of the Spirit went out from Mary into Elizabeth's heart.

Now as soon as Elizabeth heard Mary's greeting, the child leapt in her womb and Elizabeth was filled with the Holy Spirit. She gave a loud cry and said, 'Of all women you are the most blessed, and blessed is the fruit of your womb. Why should I be honored with a visit from the mother of my Lord? For the moment your greeting reached my ears, the child in my womb leapt for joy. Yes, blessed is she who believed that the promise made her by the Lord would be fulfilled (Lk 1:41-45).

And Mary sang her beautiful song of victory under the inspiration of the Holy Spirit: "My soul proclaims the greatness of the Lord and my spirit exults in God my Savior, because He has looked upon His lowly handmaid" (Lk 1:46-47).

Wherever Mary went, the soft dew of God's Holy Spirit fell gently upon all, stirring the seeds of divine life within their hearts. The simple shepherds "found Mary and Joseph, and the baby lying in the manger" (Lk 2:16) and their hearts too were filled with the joy of the Holy Spirit.

And the shepherds went back glorifying and praising God for all they had heard and seen; it was exactly as they had been told (Lk 2:20).

The Magi also received an outpouring of the Spirit through the presence of Mary.

The sight of the star filled them with delight, and going into the house they saw the child with his mother Mary, and falling to their knees they did him homage. Then, opening their treasures, they offered him gifts of gold and frankincense and myrrh (Mt 2:11).

SIMEON AND ANNA

One of the most touching scenes in the Gospel is the encounter of Mary's giving Jesus to the waiting arms of the old Simeon and Anna in the Temple. Symbol of the Old Testament *Anawim*, the Remnant of God that waited expectantly for the coming of the Messiah, Simeon and Anna, by prayer and fasting, were promised by the Holy Spirit that they would not die before their eyes beheld the Savior of Israel. Mary offers Jesus to the waiting hungry world as she allows Simeon to hold the Savior and sing, his heart full of the Spirit's joy.

In the Great Vespers of the Byzantine Rite for the feast of the Presentation of Jesus in the Temple, the Church sings:

> Today Simeon, the ancient, enters the Temple rejoicing in the Spirit to receive in his arms the Lawgiver and Fulfiller of the law of Moses. Whereas Moses was accounted worthy to be a man who saw God through darkness and in a voice not manifested and who with his covered face reproved the unfaithful hearts of the Jews, Simeon carried the Ever-existent and Incarnate Word of the Father and has opened unto the Gentiles the light, the cross and resurrection. Anna, the prophetess, also showed herself, preaching the Savior, the Deliverer of Israel. Let us cry unto Him, Christ, our God. For the sake of the Theotokos, have mercy on us.

The joy that Mary brought into Simeon's life was unbounded. "Now, Master, you can let Your servant go in peace, just as You promised; because my eyes have seen the Salvation which You prepared for all the nations to see. . ." (Lk 2:29). But the Holy Spirit was also given through Simeon and Anna back to Mary and Joseph as they prophesied that Mary's heart would be pierced with a sword of sorrow. By being an occasion of the Holy Spirit for Simeon, Mary also receives through Simeon a new enlightenment from the Holy Spirit. Her "fiat," made when the Holy Spirit came upon her, is becoming concretized by the Holy Spirit's first warning that Mary would have to suffer as her Son would become the sign of rejection among His people.

LIFE AT NAZARETH

Scripture gives us nothing of the Spirit-giving occasions that occurred in Mary's life at Nazareth in her relationships with her relatives, friends and fellow villagers. But her solicitude at the wedding feast of Cana would lead us to imagine that she went about doing good, impelled by that inner power of the Holy Spirit's love. For one as sensitive to the presence of the Spirit, Mary must have been a quiet, loving force in Nazareth. Her radiant beauty and humility must have attracted her fellow villagers to her humble home. Her days must have been filled with gentle ways of doing good in little ways, often unnoticed by others, except the one who felt the presence of the Holy Spirit of God passing from Mary to him or to her as Mary performed some act of kindness.

"WOMAN, BEHOLD THY SON"

How the Holy Spirit, through Mary's presence in their lives, must have been powerfully felt in the hearts of the

Apostles, especially St. John the Beloved Disciple to whom Jesus entrusted His mother. It was John who twice calls Mary *woman*. In describing Mary's intercession with Jesus at the wedding feast at Cana, John presents Mary, not only as the physical mother of Christ, but also as the spiritual mother of the Mystical Body—the Church. At the Cross, John heard those words from the dying Jesus: "Woman, this is your son. . . .This is your mother" (Jn 19:26). He received an infusion of the Holy Spirit, not only to love Mary as his very own mother, to see that all of her needs were provided for, but to see Mary as the Universal Mother Church, and himself as representative of her children.

We cannot imagine what a source of strength and consolation Mary's presence to the Apostles and early Christians was by way of mediating, in her silent way, the Holy Spirit. The Acts shows Mary in the center of the Apostles and other followers.

In Vatican II's *Constitution on the Church*, Mary's role in that early Christian community is described in these words:

> But since it has pleased God not to manifest solemnly the mystery of the salvation of the human race before He would pour forth the Spirit promised by Christ, we see the Apostles before the day of Pentecost "persevering with one mind in prayer with the women and Mary the Mother of Jesus and with His brethren," and Mary by her prayers imploring the gift of the Spirit, who had already overshadowed her in the Annunciation (no. 59).

Mary had pondered all the many things that had been foretold about her Son Jesus, keeping them in her heart. Now after the Ascension she must have shared many of the joys that were hers in the years of living so intimately with

Jesus at Nazareth. If the Holy Spirit is the bond of unity that brings members of the Body of Christ more closely together, Mary surely had a great role to play in that early Christian community by her quiet presence that released the Holy Spirit in greater abundance in the hearts of all that came into contact with her. That community grew in wisdom and charity, unfolding as Mary the first Christian unfolded at Nazareth because the Holy Spirit was upon her. St. Luke tells us of that Jerusalem Christian community:

> These remained faithful to the teaching of the Apostles, to the brotherhood, to the breaking of bread and to the prayers....The faithful all lived together and owned everything in common; they sold their goods and possessions and shared out the proceeds among themselves according to what each one needed. They went as a body to the Temple every day but met in their houses for the breaking of bread; they shared their food gladly and generously; they praised God and were looked up to by everyone. Day by day the Lord added to their community those destined to be saved (Acts 2:42-47).

MARY BAPTIZED BY THE HOLY SPIRIT

Before His Ascension, Jesus promised Mary and His Disciples: "...you shall be baptized with the Holy Spirit not many days hence" (Acts 1:5). If Mary on Pentecost received an outpouring of the Holy Spirit with the gifts and fruit of the Spirit given to her and to the Disciples of Jesus, it would not be difficult to believe that Mary, both before, and above all every day after Pentecost, yielded completely to the indwelling Holy Spirit. Every true

Christian has the indwelling of the Holy Spirit but not every believer is *controlled* by the Spirit of Jesus.

Mary, in a process from her first awareness of herself in relationship to God, ever grew in faith, obedience and love of God's indwelling Spirit. "It is the Spirit that gives life; the flesh profits nothing" (Jn 6:63). It is the Holy Spirit within Mary that makes her not only the Mother of Jesus but also the perfect Christian, the Mother who serves to bring forth the Word of God within the heart of every human being.

Of all Christians, who ever brought forth—in service to the Body of Christ—more fruit of the Holy Spirit than Mary?

> What the Spirit brings is very different: love, joy, peace, patience, kindness, goodness, trustfulness, gentleness and self control. . . .Since the Spirit is our life, let us be directed by the Spirit (Ga 5:22-25).

Of all the proofs of the submission of Mary to the indwelling Holy Spirit, none is greater than the love produced in her life by the Spirit. All other fruits and gifts of the Holy Spirit are mere manifestations of the one *Gift*, the Spirit Himself, who is given to Mary and to all true believing Christians. ". . .the love of God has been poured into our hearts by the Holy Spirit which has been given to us" (Rm 5:5). The Heavenly Father brings forth His Son in Mary through His Spirit of love.

But Mary experienced what John, the beloved disciple, had so beautifully described:

> No one has ever seen God;
> but as long as we love one another
> God will live in us

And His love will be complete in us.
We can know that we are living in Him
And He is living in us
because He lets us share His Spirit. . . .
God is love
and anyone who lives in love lives in God,
and God lives in him. . . .
So this is the commandment that He has given us,
that anyone who loves God must also love his brother
  (1 Jn 4:12-21).

She was dominated by God's love. All her other virtues, including her great infused knowledge and understanding and wisdom were permeated by the Spirit's love in her. The gifts that St. Paul describes in 1 Co 12 are manifestations of the one Spirit who most perfectly expresses His presence by expressing His inner nature—the love of God toward others in self-giving. Without love, all other gifts of the Spirit in Mary would be meaningless. Informed by the Spirit's love, all other gifts have meaning in building up the Body of Christ.

Concretely Mary's love for all persons that she met in her lifetime was always patient and kind; never jealous, never boastful or conceited; never rude or selfish. It took no offense and was not resentful. It was always ready to excuse, to trust, to hope and to endure whatever came. Her love never came to an end (1 Co 13).

EVER-EXPANDING CONSCIOUSNESS

In a word, Mary's relationship to the Holy Spirit was one of ever-increasing docility and surrender to the deifying power of the Spirit. The work of the Spirit in

Mary is to lead her continually, as He does in all human beings created by God for contemplating God in all things, to ever new levels of awareness of her oneness in the Trinity with the whole created world outside herself.

She receives, as she cooperates with the Spirit, a greater and greater infusion of faith, hope and love to experience God as Abba. She "sees" the indescribable tenderness of the Father that makes her, through His Spirit of love, His daughter. She "hears" the enchantments of the Word proceeding from the Father and claiming her as mother and spouse. She "tastes" the sweetness of the Spirit's love from the Father and the Son, vivifying her and exalting her as blessed above all generations.

With St. Augustine, Mary, the temple of the Holy Spirit, could cry out:

> What is it that I love, my God, when I love Thee? It is not a sensible beauty. . .nor the melodies of a varied song nor the sweet odor of flowers nor the taste of manna nor bodily caresses. No, it is none of these things that I love in my God. And yet, what I love in Him is a certain light, sound, odor, food, embrace, which can be experienced only in the interior. My soul sees a light shine which is not contained in space; it hears a sound which is not diminished by time; it smells a perfume which is not carried by the air; it tastes a food which neither diminishes nor pales.[6]

MYSTICAL UNION WITH THE TRINITY

Continually, through the infusion of mystical gifts of contemplation, Mary grew in her burning desire to love and serve God, to be completely absorbed in God and filled with Him. She felt herself as entirely in God, being surrounded and possessed by Him. She experienced her emptiness being filled with the infinite riches of God's love. The faith given her by the Holy Spirit seems to yield in its darkness to an inner blazing light. God is "seen" in such a powerful experience as a light that makes her "light from Light."

At the foot of the Cross especially did Mary experience the final purification of the Holy Spirit. We do not always fully realize the powerful love-activities of the Holy Spirit within the hearts of Christians to whom God wishes to give Himself, even in this life, in a transforming union. The highest union of any Christian mystic must have been attained by Mary through the Holy Spirit. Although sinless, as the Church has taught for 2,000 years, Mary, in the deepest regions of her consciousness and unconscious, needed to be divinized by a divine transformation that passed through the crucible of the darkness of sorrows, weakness, adversities, calumnies, interior sterility and desolation. As she saw her Son hanging on the Cross, "as someone punished, struck by God and brought low" (Is 53:4), she too knew a terrifying sense of annihilation and abandonment by God.

She wrung from the depths of her being, through the power of the Holy Spirit's faith, hope and love within her, her renewed "fiat." "Be it done to me according to Your Word!" The Heavenly Father submerged her into an ocean of terrifying darkness and bitterness. The unifying, transforming power of the Holy Spirit brought Mary into a new level of oneness with the Father, Son and Holy Spirit that was in proportion to her sorrows.

I need only say, "I am slipping," and your love, Yahweh, immediately and in the middle of all my troubles supports me; You console me and make me happy (Ps 94:18-19).

The greatest joy that the Spirit infused into Mary was to allow her to be purified of her nothingness and filled with joyful humility. She thus experienced the oneness of God's essence as Love within her and at the same time the inexpressible mystery of the unique relationships of Father to Son in the Spirit, reproduced in the depths of her being.

Still she grew daily in this transforming union with God as One and as Three. What the Spirit revealed to her as an inner experience of the Holy Trinity living and loving within her, she also experienced as the same Holy Trinity living and loving in God's uncreated energies within each creature. Mary's life on earth, continued in her heavenly state, was one of humble service as a purified channel of God's love toward all creatures.

Her death was not an horrendous wrenching from a vision of imperfect faith, over the darkness and uncertainty that lie on the other side of death's portal, but rather a yielding to the Spirit's light, "from glory to glory."

> . . .for the effects of the light are seen in complete goodness and right living and truth. . .anything exposed by the light will be illuminated and anything illuminated turns into light. That is why it is said: "Wake up from your sleep, rise from the dead, and Christ will shine on you" (Ep 5:9-14).

The Byzantine Christians thus preferred to call Mary's demise, *koimisis*, a dormition, a restful sleep, a repose rather than a death.

St. John Damascene writes on the feast of Mary's Assumption:

> Wherefore we shall not call your holy departure death, but a lying down to sleep or a going abroad, or better still, a

homecoming. For leaving the things of the body, you enter into the possession of better things.[7]

MARY – THE SPIRIT'S MASTERPIECE

God's Spirit came upon Mary, not only when she conceived God's Word in her womb, but Christians from the earliest times believed that the same Spirit protected her from the very beginning of her earthly existence. Mary is what we are to become. But Mary is still becoming the Holy Spirit's masterpiece as she yields in perfect obedience to His deifying, transforming power. Her relationship to the Spirit is not through one or other gift received but consists in the highest reaches of human consciousness of God's supreme dominance in her life, of her own utter poverty before such holiness and of her ecstatic union in love of the One and the Three, in which union she finds her uniqueness and praises God's election of her as blessed of Yahweh who has looked with mercy upon His handmaid's lowliness. She reverences the presence of the One and the Three in each part of the created world and she cries out with joyful self-giving: "Behold Your servant; do with me whatever You wish. That You may be glorified. That Your kingdom come. That Your Son and my Son may be acclaimed as Lord of the Universe. That your Spirit may be loved as You and Your Son love each other. Amen! Amen! Glory to God in the highest!"

MARY WAS A MEADOW

Mary was a meadow for the Lord
Mary was His rich and fertile plain
Mary was the planted field, Jesus was the seed,

Jesus is the harvest yield
to fill our every need—
Mary make my life a fertile plain
reap in me your rare and golden grain.

Mary was a crystal for the Lord
Mary was the prism of His light
Mary was the windowed wall, Jesus was the ray,
Jesus is the rainbow fall
to cheer our every day—
Mary be my crystal for the light
hold Him ever glowing in my sight.

Mary was a woodwind for the Lord
Mary was His pure and tranquil tone
Mary was the perfect key, Jesus was the song,
Jesus is the melody for all to sing along—
Mary make my love a perfect tone
that my heart may sing for God alone.

Bill Peffley

5

Mary Holy

God is a sacramental God. He deigns to become present to us with His uncreated energies by using material signs. He humbly consents to work through such signs. The greatest sacramental sign that God has chosen in which to be present to us human beings is the humanity of Jesus Christ. His materiality, a human body that could speak, could love, could touch and heal and forgive, becomes the prime source of all other sacramental encounters.

Christ would extend His glorified Body's contact with us through the sacramental actions of the Church, His Mystical Body. Under the symbolic signs of bread and wine He gives Himself to us as our food. Water allows Him to cleanse us of sin, oil soothes the wounds, salt purifies, the touch of human hands, spoken words by human lips provide the Risen Lord Jesus with means to be present with His divinizing power. The religion of Jesus Christ is sacramental and uses material signs to bring us into his holy redeeming presence. This flows from the vision that He had of His Heavenly Father working always in every atom of this universe. In the scene of the cure of the cripple at the Probatic Pool, Jesus defends His healing action against the apparent violation of God's law to keep sacred the Sabbath by stating: "My Father goes on working, and so do I" (Jn 5:17). Jesus sees His Father always present and working in and through His own material creation to build up in a transforming process the Kingdom of Heaven. Especially is this gracious Father working in the world of men and women throughout all of human history. God is in human history and is a guiding presence.

MARY – A SIGN OF GOD'S HOLINESS

When the Heavenly Father's love reaches its fullest manifestation in His Word becoming flesh and dwelling among us in human form, Jesus becomes in His humanity the sign of the Father's holiness and goodness. "He is the image of the unseen God" (Col 1:15). Philip at the Last Supper spoke for all of us: "Lord, let us see the Father and then we shall be satisfied" (Jn 14:8). But Jesus tells all of us: "To have seen Me is to have seen the Father. . .I am in the Father and the Father is in me. . .it is the Father living in Me who is doing this work" (Jn 14:9-10).

Jesus is the Image of the Father and according to this Image we have all been created (Gn 1:26). Yet God's holiness in Jesus is still too awesome. He is still God, the eternal pre-existing Logos. God gives us a human sign, an image that has come into existence as a quantified person in matter. Mary is the image or sign of what God has destined us human beings to become in Christ Jesus.

Now a great sign appeared in Heaven: a woman, adorned with the sun, standing on the moon, and with the twelve stars on her head for a crown (Rv 12:1).

At the beginning of His restoration of the human race to its original grandeur and dignity that Adam and Eve had lost by sin, God raised up Mary as the sign of perfect human holiness to which we are all called in Jesus Christ. She was "adorned from the first instant of her conception with the splendors of an entirely unique holiness. . ."[1] Yet she, like us, was in need of the redeeming grace of the only Mediator, Jesus Christ. ". . .because she belongs to the offspring of Adam, she is one with all human beings in their need for salvation."[2]

Mary is God's preview, as it were, of what we human beings by God's grace can hope to become. She comes as the first Christian, the first human being who is totally conscious that Jesus Christ lives in her, and she surrenders totally in faith and loving obedience to serve Him. She is the beginning of the Church, an individual or a collectivity of individuals in whom Christ's Spirit dwells and operates to produce His fruit of love, peace and joy, the signs of the Church among men. She is in a miniature form what the whole Church will become by God's divinizing grace.

Her holiness is unique insofar as God poured out His sanctifying Spirit upon her from her first moment of existence. Yet it all points to God's free gift of His encompassing love that is of the same nature as His loving grace given to us.

Karl Rahner compares the difference between the graces of holiness that Mary received and our own gifts:

> Mary does not differ from us because she possessed these gifts. It is her possession of them from the beginning, and incomparably, that is the sole difference between her and us. As for the content of this gift, its nature and intrinsic meaning, the eternal Father could not intend anything for the mother of

His incarnate Son, without intending it for us too, and giving it to us in the sacrament of justification.

For us, too, He eternally intended this saving grace from the beginning, in His temporal life, in order that it might be plain that it is all His grace, that nothing in our salvation belongs to us of ourselves. God has eternally kept His eternal love in readiness for us too, so that in the moment that we call our baptism, He may come into the depths of our heart. For we too are redeemed, saved, marked with God's indelible seal. We too have been made the holy temple of God. In us too the triune God dwells. We too have been sent by Him, from this beginning, into our life, that we too may carry the light of faith and the flame of love through this world's faith and the flame of love through this world's darkness, to the place where we belong in His eternal radiance, His eternity.3

THE HOLINESS OF MARY

The Holy Spirit has given to Christians throughout the centuries an understanding of Mary's holiness in a consciousness that gradually unfolded and centered around two central points: that Mary was freed of original sin by the merits of Jesus Christ in the first moment of her conception and that she grew in grace and holiness through cooperating with the Spirit's gifts of faith, hope and love so that she remained all her lifetime sinless and holy.

We can see in Mary's life, even as we see in our own, the full gratuitous gift of redemption offered her, not because she had merited it but purely out of God's free decree. God redeems Mary, not for herself but for us that she might be of service in building up the Body of Christ. She receives such outstanding gifts that put her from the very beginning of her conception under God's protective love because God predestined her to greater service in the Church.

Mary's holiness is ultimately our belief and hope that, as Mary through the Holy Spirit was always in Christ, so we since our Baptism have been in Him and growing by our daily cooperation with His love and grace to approach her union with Christ. Mary in popular Christian devotion is the Star of the Sea. Her spiritual perfection shines like a beacon to all of us as we battle the darkness of the sea and its sudden tempestuous storms to move ever closer to the goal of our life. We are called to reach her holiness. By God's grace she is what God wants all of us to become.

HOLINESS – A GROWTH PROCESS

Holiness is not a static moment given to Mary in her conception. For her it consists in a process of discovering that God's love has truly surrounded and completely penetrated her. She had to push her consciousness, always by the power of the Holy Spirit, to new levels of awareness that God was Allness and she was emptiness, filled by God's gift of love. The "Remnant" of the Israelites in exile, the *Anawim* of the desert, focused to a point of greatest intensity in Mary. Each day of Mary's life was a growth in experiencing what Sophonias described:

> But I will leave as a remnant in your midst a people humble and lowly, who shall take refuge in the name of the Lord: the remnant of Israel. They shall do no wrong and speak no lies; nor shall there be found in their mouths a deceitful tongue (Soph 3:11-13).

In her poverty and humility, Mary gradually grew in a surrendering adoration that was actualized by her fidelity to do at all times God's holy will in her regard. She was filled with the holy fear and reverence for Yahweh's awesome presence. Yet she knew His sweetness. Not only was the holiness of the Old Testament known to Mary in her prayerful study of God's Word but she became that holiness by a continued experience of greater intensity. How beautifully the Psalmist outlines such a holiness:

> I sought the Lord and He answered me
> and delivered me from all my fears.
> Look to Him that you may be radiant with joy
> and your faces may not blush with shame.
> When the afflicted man called out, the Lord heard
> and from all his distress He saved him.
> The angel of the Lord encamps
> around those who fear Him and delivers them.
> Taste and see how good the Lord is;
> happy the man who takes refuge in Him.
> Fear the Lord, you His holy ones
> for naught is lacking to those who fear Him.
> The great grow poor and hungry;
> but those who seek the Lord want for no good thing.
> The Lord has eyes for the just
> and ears for their cry.
> When the just cry out, the Lord hears them
> and from all their distress He rescues them.
> The Lord is close to the brokenhearted;
> and those who are crushed in spirit He saves (Ps 33:4-19).

Mary's holiness unfolded in the context of her daily life. She *became* full of grace by yielding herself to the promptings of God's Spirit. Like us, she too had to cooperate with God's grace at each moment of her life.

THE CHURCH'S CONSCIOUSNESS OF HER HOLINESS

As Mary's growth in holiness developed through her deepened consciousness of God's dominance in her life, so in a similar manner we can see in the history of the Church a growth process in greater consciousness of Mary's perfect holiness. Unless we can see the Holy Spirit leading the faithful from an implicit belief in Mary's sanctity that becomes more explicit as the Church ponders upon this aspect of Mary, we shall be shocked to discover the varying positions taken in this matter in the early centuries.

It was Cardinal John Henry Newman who worked out a theory of doctrinal development that allows us to investigate the Church's consciousness concerning Mary's holiness and to see a growth process. Faith for him is a concrete intuition of supernatural realities, a vision, at times unconscious even to the persons perceiving it. Thus a supernatural truth can remain implicit in the minds of individuals and, therefore, of the Church for centuries without formal expression, and yet develop by means of unconscious, spontaneous, implicit reasoning, at the same time nourishing the devotion and piety of the faithful.[4] The problems that Mary was conceived without original sin (the dogma of the Immaculate Conception) and that she remained sinless all of her life were posed in the early Church as the problem of her sanctity.

BEFORE THE COUNCIL OF EPHESUS (431)

Before the Council of Ephesus which defined that Mary was the *Theotokos*, the Mother of God, and hence gave new impetus to speculation about the prerogatives of

Mary that flowed properly from this established dogma, the Fathers of the Church show mixed attitudes toward the Holy Virgin. At some time there was an exasperatingly indifferent attitude, at other times an outright attribution of human failings and defects or a gradual type of purification and sanctification that provided her with the sanctity due to her exalted position.

In the development of doctrine where belief in the Church moves gradually (and at times even imperceptibly) from an implicit to an explicit belief, theologians distinguish various steps. In the first phase the teaching body grasps an idea, various members taking different aspects or viewpoints of the same fundamental idea. Then there follows a period in which proponents of imperfect interpretations and understandings of the idea clash with one another. The idea is gradually delineated, the conflict ends and the third phase begins with the idea now fixed in the Church's consciousness. The fourth and final phase climaxes in the acceptance by each believer of the idea as his own and a part of revealed truth.[5]

The period before the Council of Ephesus was a period of clarification of the great Christological teachings concerning the Incarnation and Redemption, with Our Lady intimately connected with Christ's saving role as the New Adam. We have already seen how the Fathers, especially the Asiatic and Palestinian, developed their teaching of Mary through their analogy of Mary as the New Eve. There emerge two fundamental Marian teachings that Mary is truly the Mother of the Word made flesh and she remains always the virgin, gradually conceived as the *holy* virgin.

In the positive progression toward a fuller, more explicit awareness of the sanctity of Mary, the early

Fathers before Ephesus defended her holiness against the gross attacks of heretics and laid the seeds for future speculation in their analogy of Mary as the New Eve. In the second half of the second century, certain Jews and pagans sought to discredit Jesus by attacking His mother. They leveled against her the calumny that she was a woman of bad morals, a public prostitute. Tertullian repeats the attack of Celsus and others against Our Lady as having been a *quaestuaria*, a prostitute, and violently answers this.[6]

We do not have any idea of what the common reaction of early Christians was but we can infer that various apocryphal writings exalting our Lady's holiness as something bordering on the miraculous were a popular reaction to such calumnies. In the composition of the influential apocryphal *Protoevangelium of James* (150-180) we find popular piety anticipating theological speculation by presenting Our Lady's virginity and holiness, especially her own conception in the womb of St. Anne, as something quite miraculous and hence in keeping with her holy dignity in her unique mission.

Justin, in his parallel between Eve and Mary, insists that both were virgins. He does not carry through with the conclusion that would follow from his strict parallelism in each detail when he insists also that, as Eve was incorrupt at that time, so also Mary was incorrupt, stainless, all-pure. For Irenaeus, Mary is intimately united to Christ in his recapitulation of the human race back to its primitive state.

As the human race had been handed over to death through a virgin, it was equally saved through a virgin; through a perfect parallel, virginal obedience repaired that which virginal disobedience had lost.[7]

Did such Fathers connect the intimate role of Mary in the restoration or redemption of the human race as the New Eve with an exceptional degree of sanctity? The Fathers before the Nicene Council (325) never posed the question. They were interested in redemption through Christ, and Mary was viewed only in her intimate relationship to Christ.

HOLY BUT NOT SINLESS

On the other hand we find in the period before Nicea the two transitional theologians, Tertullian and Origen, preparing the ground for future patristic texts which convince us that the early patristic idea of Mary's holiness does not make her stainless in our sense of the term through our evolved doctrine of original sin. Tertullian at times turns on Mary with a rudeness that shocks us. Jesus apparently condemns her publicly because of her incredulity when He asks "Who is my mother and who are my brethren?"[8] She manifested her disbelief in His mission by staying aloof while other women, like Martha and Mary Magdalene, cooperated more closely with Him. We might be able to understand these texts when we consider that Tertullian was an outspoken, fiery polemist, already tinged by Montanism, with a penchant for degrading the female sex. But at any rate, he shows us that there was no accepted teaching to the contrary in the Church at this time.

Origen also presents texts that are hardly laudatory of Mary. He teaches in Caesarea that the sword of sorrow that

Mary experienced was the scandal that she experienced standing at the foot of the Cross of her Son. A sword of disbelief, doubt, uncertainty pierced her.[9] Similar remarks are found in these homilies which were preached to the people of Caesarea. As we have no record of a protest by his audience or higher ecclesiastical authorities, we can believe that this was the acceptable language throughout all of Palestine of which Caesarea was the capital, likewise in Egypt where his writings were widely diffused among his disciples.

Does such language indicate a lack of esteem for the Mother of God? Hardly, as Origen shows in many writings. He praises those who praise Mary for her virtues, and personally considers her as the perfect model for all Christian virgins. Yet he does not exempt her from all fault. This is undoubtedly because he focuses, as his predecessor, Clement of Alexandria, on the principle: no one has avoided in this world all sin except the Redeemer who was stainless and needed no redemption.

Thus we find that there was no unified doctrine about the perfect sanctity of Our Lady in these early centuries. Though they did attribute to her an eminent sanctity, this did not, however, exclude all weaknesses and human failings. We will see how the ascetics, broadening from the basic concept of her virginity into an all-perfect model for Christians, would develop her sinlessness to a point that would logically demand the Immaculate Conception.

Between Nicea and Ephesus, Arianism was the main preoccupation of the East. Our Lady is treated as before Nicea but now in mounting numbers of texts, both in favor of her unique holiness and in emphasis of her human failings and defects. For St. Cyril of Alexandria, the great proponent of Mary as *Theotokos* in the Council of Ephesus, in writing shortly before the Council, speaks of Mary as a saint who could have known human sin. Mary had ceased to believe in her Son as He hung on the Cross. Jesus, according to St. Cyril, gave her to St. John in order that John might help her find again faith in her Divine Son.[10] Mary at the foot of the Cross became scandalized and almost lost her own sanity. This was due to her ignorance of the mystery that her Son had to suffer and die and thus redeem the world. He links up this as a fact and not an idle speculation for thus was fulfilled the prophecy of St. Simeon whose predicted sword of sorrow was the piercing attack on her thoughts during the Passion which drove her to strange thoughts.[11]

ST. JOHN CHRYSOSTOM

But the most outspoken writer about the human defects of Our Lady is St. John Chrysostom. He explains the reason why the angel Gabriel had to tell Mary the truth about her conception:

In order to prevent confusion and trouble in her mind because, if she did not know the full truth, she could have reached some wild decision about herself, and in utter shame could have hanged herself or even stabbed herself.[12]

Commenting on the wedding at Cana, John Chrysostom, along with other patristic writers as Irenaeus, reproves Mary for her untimely haste that Jesus prove Himself as a miracle-worker, and adds that Mary "sought to gain favor with the disciples also, making herself more well-known through the deeds of her Son."[13] He imputes

the same motive of vain ambition to Mary in the scene
where she stands outside with the "brethren of Jesus."

> What she (Mary) strove to do was motivated by an excess of
> ambition; she wanted to show herself to the people as having
> complete power over her Son. At this time she did not have
> any uncommon idea about His greatness; that is why action
> was uncalled for.[14]

Many Orthodox today still hold, quoting such
Fathers as St. Cyril of Jerusalem, Gregory of Nazianzen
and Ephrem, that Our Lady was not conceived in birth
without the stain of sin but only at the Annunciation was
she gradually purified from all sin.[15] St. Cyril has the Holy
Spirit descending upon her and thus sanctifying her so as
to enable her to receive properly the Maker of all things.[16]
St. Ephrem also speaks of a gradual purification by the
Holy Spirit.[17]

In this period before Ephesus, St. Epiphanius and
St. Ephrem are the two outstanding defendants of a
unique, superior degree of holiness for the Mother of God.
For Epiphanius, Mary is not only the Holy Virgin but she
is all-full of grace.[18] We cannot draw from these statements the conclusion that Epiphanius held that Mary was
immaculately conceived without sin. The problem never
was posed that Mary should have been an exemption to
the universal law proposed by St. Paul that all men were
born in sin.

St. Ephrem, representing the Syrian school, sings
Mary's praises as higher in holiness than the Cherubim,
more lovely than the Seraphim, superior in purity to all
the choirs of angels.[19] His teaching on our Lady's sanctity
can be summarized in his exclamation to Christ:

In truth, You and Your mother, You are perfectly beautiful in all respects; for in You, Lord, there is no stain, and in Your mother there is no spot.[20]

A clear concept of original sin would be too much to ask of St. Ephrem, but at least he provides the basis for the conclusion of the Immaculate Conception centuries later when theology would have clarified St. Paul's teaching on the first sin of Adam.

WESTERN THOUGHT

In the West, devotion to Our Lady received a great impetus as virgins and ascetics enthusiastically modeled their life of greater perfection on the sanctity of Mary. Ambrose, a personal friend of St. Athanasius, to whom is credited a Coptic manuscript describing Mary as the perfect model of virgins,[21] goes so far in his enthusiasm for the sanctity of Mary as to declare that she is "a virgin freed through grace from all stain of sin."[22]

Augustine follows the thought of Ambrose in regard to Mary's virginity. Through his theological war against Pelagius, Augustine developed the basic principle of the utter gratuity of grace. Pelagius exalted Mary as freed from all sin because of his excessive optimism in human nature. Augustine insisted that if Mary avoided all sin, it was due purely to divine favor and her intimate relation with the Savior.[23] Here there is question in Augustine's mind of Mary's perfect holiness in regard to personal sin, but his adversary, Julian of Eclanum, made Augustine face the issue of original sin. Julian wanted no man to be under its stain and complained about Augustine: "You have done worse than Jovinian. He dissolved the virginity of Mary by subjecting her to the normal conditions of childbearing; but you hand over Mary to the devil by submitting her to the conditions of human generation." For Julian Our Lady would have been under the stain of original sin by the mere fact of the universality of the law of sin that was handed on through human procreation. She could have avoided it only by having been virginally conceived as was Christ. Augustine answered this attack toward the end of his life when he had developed clearly his thought on original sin. Yet his answer would be a barrier toward further development of the doctrine of the Immaculate Conception. "We do not surrender Mary to the power of the devil by subjecting her to the condition of human generation but because the very condition of human generation is abrogated by grace of her rebirth."[24]

The Middle Ages would split into two camps on the interpretation of this. One would interpret Augustine's statement as meaning what we would later mean by the Immaculate Conception, namely, that Mary was simply from the first moment of her existence through a special grace freed from the stain that was inherited by every man through human procreation. The rigorists interpreted this as though Mary were born as any other human being, in original sin, but gradually was purified and freed from the stain and the effects.

We could ask ourselves: how are so many texts reconcilable with a belief that should have been at least implicit in the early Church? We must always keep in mind that the absence of universal belief does not constitute therein a rejection of that belief. Many Fathers did express, but often in analogical, poetical language, belief in Mary's unique sanctity. Other Fathers seemed to ignore it.

Indifference does not mean belief to the contrary. But in the cases that we have seen of texts that impute human faults to Mary or that insist on a gradual purification, how can we reconcile these with the future development of teaching on the Immaculate Conception?

ONLY CHRIST WITHOUT SIN

The Fathers were staying literally with Holy Scripture, especially St. Paul, in maintaining that only Jesus Christ remained without sin. In this general form we must also hold this truth, namely, that only God is impeccable by His very nature. Sin in God would be a contradiction. Sin is the turning away from God, the loss of divine life. But the Fathers, who generally were interested in Christological developments rather than Marian theology as a special point of speculation, never denied the distinction that innocence or impeccability could be granted, as St. Augustine insisted against Pelagius, by a superior grace.

In regard to the many patristic texts of exegesis we must remember that the Fathers were often giving an oratorical exegesis that was arbitrary and, according to the majority of New Testament exegetes, even in those days, inadmissible. That she asked for an explanation of Archangel Gabriel in the Annunciation was dictated by her prudence and humility. The sword that pierced her heart at the foot of the Cross was produced by her complete sorrow and anxiety, not to a lack of faith in the divinity of her Son. But in all these texts we must remember that the Fathers express these human frailties of Our Lady usually not as anything deliberate or culpable. But for those Fathers who admitted in Mary true, actual faults, would this imply that they implicitly recognized that she was born with original sin? Cardinal Newman, in an essay touching this question,[25] maintains that these human imperfections were not considered real effects of original sin. The Fathers before Augustine never probed this problem and when they did discuss the effects of Adam's fall in human posterity, it was to view these effects in terms of death, corruption and darkness, in a constant movement away from God.

Before Ephesus we can say that the Fathers, in dealing with the universality of original sin and the need of universal redemption, were not yet preoccupied with an exception. In any organic development, the universal must be developed first, in this case the universal law of original sin and redemption imposed on the human race. But they did not yet deduce from their other analogies of Our Lady in her role of cooperating with Christ in the redemption of the human race that in the application of this universal law there could be an exception which would not destroy the universality of the law.

GRADUAL PURIFICATION

For the Fathers, such as Ephrem, Cyril of Jerusalem and Gregory of Nazianzen, who apparently advocated a gradual purification in the soul of Mary, would this be in contradiction to any further development of her perfect sanctity? In their exegesis of Luke 1:35, "And the Holy Spirit will overshadow you. . ." it can be explained that Our Lady did actually receive an increase in sanctifying grace, that she actually grew in grace, actually became holier, which would not in the least imply a purification from the stain of original or any personal sin. Mary was full of grace, but this, viewed as the Life of God living and acting in her soul, admitted of growth, a progressive movement away from darkness, corruption, death, toward Life itself, Light, Incorruption. We find such Fathers influenced by Pseudo-Dionysius in his teaching on the hierarchical purification of angels.[26]

AFTER THE COUNCIL OF EPHESUS

Against Nestorius, the Fathers of Ephesus fought for the title of Mother of God. This focused theological speculation on her virginal maternity and highlighted her sublime sanctity as befitting her dignity of Mother of God. In the West the rigorist interpretation of Augustine began to form a barrier that would last for centuries against any further development. Yet in the East, after Ephesus, we find the liturgical development of a cultus to Mary through the establishment of an annual cycle of Marian feasts to commemorate the principal events of her life. This gave impetus to the Oriental homily in which orators and poets rivaled in proclaiming the glories of Mary. Usually the language used provides us with strong implicit testimony of their growing awareness that Mary was all-pure and all-holy. But, except for a few cases, these expressions were not formulated into theological concepts that would approximate our own present terminology.

St. Andrew of Crete best summarizes the Church's thinking in the East after the Council of Ephesus on Our Lady's holiness. He bases the sublime sanctity and purity of Mary on the fact that Mary was chosen to be the Mother of the New Man, therefore her conception and

birth were holy. God intervened in a particular manner in
the miraculous conception of Mary because, not only was
she to give birth to the Son of God, but she herself was
destined by God to be the first fruits of restored
humanity; she was to reflect in her person the pristine
beauty of the human race.[27] In his eight Marian homilies
and two canons composed for the feast of the Conception
of St. Anne and the Nativity of Our Lady we find
innumerable phrases that come the closest to our concept
of the Immaculate Conception. He writes:

> Today Adam offers Mary to God in our name as the first fruits
> of our nature. . . .Today humanity in all the brilliance of its
> immaculate, noble birth receives the gift of its first formation
> through the divine hands and refinds its pristine splendor. . . .
> Ever since the Mother of the Beautiful One was born, this
> nature has recovered in her its ancient privileges; she was
> fashioned according to a perfect model and truly one worthy
> of God. And this formation is a perfect restoration; this
> restoration is a divinization; this divinization is an assimilation
> to the primitive state. . . .In Mary the old world receives the
> first fruits of the second creation.[28]
>
> The body of the Virgin is an earth that God has cultivated,
> the first fruits of the race of Adam which has been divinized in
> Christ, the image perfectly resembling the pristine beauty.[29]

The death of Our Lady offers Andrew a difficulty. If
she is the first fruits of a new humanity, she would not be
subjected to the law of death. And if she were not
subjected to death as the wages of the sin of Adam, then it
must be because she was conceived without original sin.
From Andrew's pen for the feast of the Conception of
St. Anne, December 9, comes the phrase repeated in the
Latin feast of the Immaculate Conception: "You are all

beautiful, o my friend, you are all beautiful and there is nothing reprehensible in you."[30]

AN EVOLVED CONSCIOUSNESS

What has been already said should allow us to make the following conclusions. The idea of Our Lady's supereminent sanctity can hardly be called an explicitly revealed dogma that had been explicitly taught in the early Church. On the contrary, as in the case of many other dogmas explicitly formulated in later ecumenical councils or alone on the infallible authority of the Vicar of Christ, giving expression to the common teaching held by the whole episcopal body, this teaching is seen as a seed planted in the early Church's consciousness. Only through various circumstances over long centuries is this consciousness brought to a point of common acceptance by all the faithful as an essential part of the deposit of faith.

Agents of this progress were predominantly the ascetics and the moral preachers who held out the virginity of our Lady as a model of Christian imitation. We saw how the virginity of our Lady for the early Christians was more than the physiological state but was equivalent to saying sanctity or holiness. Though there was no connection between virginity and holiness, yet the two became synonymous in the early Church's attitude toward Mary. In this environment, under the pen of Athanasius, Ambrose, Augustine, Epiphanius, Sophronius and Andrew of Crete, Mary, the second Eve, was depicted as holy, all-holy, immaculate, freed of all stain. It would only remain for the medieval theologians, as Duns Scotus, to summarize what these earlier Fathers had been saying implicitly, without drawing the final conclusion, when he formulated his argument of convenience: "Deus potuit, decuit, fecit." (God could have done it; it was befitting to do it; therefore He did it.)

We can thus see from what has been presented above that the Church moved from a vaguely implicit, general truth held by areas of the early Church to an ever more conscious understanding that Mary was not only sinless and holy but that God had raised her up to a unique dignity of having been under the power of His Holy Spirit, in grace, freed of original sin, however the formulation be phrased. Greater clarity in theological conclusions filtered down to feed the devotion and piety of the faithful, climaxing finally in the dogmatic pronouncement of the teaching body of the Catholic Church a century ago.

CHARACTERISTICS OF MARY'S HOLINESS

By reflecting on the picture we find of Mary in Holy Scripture and guided by tradition, especially in popular and liturgical piety, we can draw out some of the appealing elements of Mary's holiness.

One characteristic of Mary's holiness is summed up in the simple word: *contentment.* Contentment is the opposite of a physical, psychical and spiritual *nervousness.* Such restless nervousness usually flows from a faulty relationship between man and God.

Mary enjoyed from earliest childhood a contentment that was a result of the Holy Spirit's gifts of deep, abiding faith, trust and love toward God. She knew she was guided in all events of her life by the powerful hands of a loving God-Father. She was moved by the Spirit to experience

God as Abba, Father (Rm 8:16; Ga 4:6). She was content with each moment for her Heavenly Father was continually manifesting Himself in the present "now."

> We know that by turning everything to their good God cooperates with all those who love Him, with all those that He has called according to His purpose. They are the ones He chose specially long ago and intended to become true images of His Son so that His Son might be the eldest of many brothers. He called those He intended for this; those He called He justified, and with those He justified He shared His glory (Rm 8:28-30).

Before her Divine Son had preached about the loving care of the Heavenly Father (Mt 6:26-30; Lk 12:22-31), Mary experienced the peace and joy that came into her life from living a life of constant abandonment in loving trust to the Heavenly Father. The Greek Fathers called this childlike confidence in the Heavenly Father *parrhesia*, not one virtue, but a way of life, a state of being before the Father that flows from the ontological, new nature that the Holy Spirit works in the heart of the baptized Christian. Mary enjoyed such a trusting confidence in each event of her life.

St. Paul could have been describing, not only his own, but also Mary's attitude toward life's situations when he wrote:

> I have learned to manage on whatever I have, I know how to be poor and I know how to be rich too. I have been through my initiation and now I am ready for anything anywhere: full stomach or empty stomach, poverty or plenty. There is nothing I cannot master with the help of the One who gives me strength (Ph 4:11-13).

Mary learned to trust in Yahweh and to live in His peace. "Commit your fate to Yahweh, trust in Him and He will act" (Ps 37:3-5). She was filled with joy and for all things she gave thanks to God (1 Th 5:18). She was the happiest of all human beings for her strength was completely in God her Savior. She felt His sustaining power upholding her in her poverty as the eagle's pinions hold up the weak eaglet that seeks to fly only under the supporting strength of the mother-eagle (Dt 32:11).

Mary's joy was not dependent upon the circumstances in which she found herself. Whether it was fleeing from the vengeful sword of Herod's soldiers in exile to Egypt or scorned by those who mocked her crucified Son on Calvary, Mary remained always "content," always filled with joy because her strength was in God. Happiness can be a fleeting thing. We do not need to be happy to be content, but no one, including Mary, was ever content without being joyful. She teaches us not to run from the situation that brings us suffering, but to find contentment with that situation.

Her contentment was built upon her vision of God working in all events of her life. "My Father goes on working, and so do I" (Jn 5:18). This developed in her a profound hope. Hope recognizes in Mary her own weakness. It places all her strength in God's goodness and holiness. Hope in God for Mary produced a reverence that allowed God perfect freedom to do with His servant Mary whatever He wanted. Mary's hope makes her wait for God's richness to be poured into her emptiness whenever and wherever He wishes. God is all and Mary knows that alone she is nothing. But her poverty before God is her true riches. ". . .He has looked upon His lowly hand-maid. . .the Almighty has done great things for me. . . .He has exalted the lowly. The hungry He has filled with good things" (Lk 1:48-53).

Mary was content and filled with joy at all times because in her littleness, in her truthful stance before the greatness of God, she continually experienced that "...anyone who humbles himself will be exalted" (Mt 23:12). God turns away from the proud, but He gives His grace to those who are humble (Jm 4:6). God delights in Mary because she is authentically what He wants all human beings to be.

MARY MOST HUMAN

It is interesting to note that as our devotion to Mary made her more angelic than human, so our appreciation of Christian holiness was all too often at the cost of depreciating the human. Jesus was truly God, completely divine. We confessed also that He was truly human, but we felt uncomfortable watching Him being touched by prostitutes, fearing in the Garden of Gethsemani, in a word, evolving into a fully realized human nature through a slow process of interpersonal relationships.

Mary indeed evolved into holiness through the human situations in which she discovered the providential love of the Heavenly Father working. We are left with no details of her childhood or growth up to the Annunciation. We can only imagine what she must have experienced as she found herself falling in love with young Joseph. As she moved toward a deeper human love for him, she discovered more of God's loveliness in Joseph. His strong body, supple yet tender, gave to her a "holy" revelation of God unobtainable in any other way. She found God's love in his pure love and self-sacrifice for her.

God is always communicating Himself as love in each human relationship. Mary opened herself to the inner beauty of God's loving presence in her love toward each person to whom she related. She came alive and discovered God inside each human encounter. Her faith allowed Mary to find God's loving presence everywhere. Her trust allowed her to give herself to the human situation without fear or nervousness. God's Spirit of love allowed her to be delicately open and sensitive to the needs of others.

"Happy the pure in heart; they shall see God" (Mt 5:8). This earth has never seen a vessel as pure as Mary. We can say that we will never see a more "human" person than Mary. She saw reality as closely as God sees it. God infused into her a purified vision that permitted Mary to see the "insideness" of God's presence. She reverenced that presence and humbly strove to serve God's will in each circumstance.

Our devotion to Mary has stressed in times past her purity. What the Holy Spirit is moving us to appreciate in Mary is her humanness, her growth in faith that necessitated vital contacts with a material world, with real men, women and children that have bodies and passions, moods and depressions. As she gave herself to God in each person, her knowledge and understanding and wisdom of God, of herself and of mankind grew. Nazareth was important to Mary's growth in contemplation. Each person in that village allowed her to meet God in him or her and thus opened Mary to meet God in all human beings.

We cannot imagine that Mary traveled much beyond Galilee and Judea, within the confines of Palestine. She surely did not give herself to great crowds of people of disparate needs and backgrounds. But her growth in humanness and holiness was determined by her freedom to be opened totally to the God-presence in each human encounter. Mary's holiness was not developed by running away from the material world or in spite of it but precisely *in* that diaphanous, material world that presented to her purified gaze God at the heart of matter.

MARY FREED TO LOVE

The holiness of Mary is the fullness of God's formation of His people, Israel. She is the culmination of the Old Testament holiness and the end of Christian sanctity, even though she represents the Church at its beginning.

God's Spirit worked in the Old Testament believers by a gradual process of purification and education. In a way, Mary is the flowering of this spiritual education of the Chosen People. The Exodus experience was more than a physical passing-over the Red Sea from Egypt into the desert and finally the entrance into the Promised Land. It was a spiritual "leading out" (*educare*) of the Jewish people from their very crude ideas of God to a loving, involved Spouse. It was a long pilgrimage away from the idols of the Egyptians, Chanaanites and Babylonians to the Holy of Holies that dwelt in the inner *Sanctum* of the Temple of Jerusalem.

Mary comes at the end of this process of purification. She was fully the daughter of Israel, praising God because He had been faithful to Abraham and to his posterity. Yet she is a new direction given to the Chosen People of Israel. Not by blood or circumcision alone would one become a member of Abraham's posterity but by a spiritual poverty and humility to serve God in a *universal* love for all mankind. Mary became a true Jew by so complete a surrender of herself to God that she becomes what Israel had been called to be: a suffering servant that the whole world might receive God's revelation of His love for all mankind.

Mary was, to use St. Paul's analogy, Sarah, the free woman, the sign of the Heavenly Jerusalem, in contrast to Agar, the slave woman, the sign of the Jewish nation enslaved by law. Entering into an ever-deepening awareness that she was a child of the Heavenly Father through the power of the Holy Spirit that overshadowed her constantly freed Mary to be the freest human being this world will ever see. For she at all times strove, not to fulfill merely the Law, but to be the servant of the Lord. She shows us that Christian freedom is an ongoing gift to us by the Holy Spirit. Freedom is to obey God, to take our whole life in hand and dispose it totally in loving service to God. True freedom is not concerned so much with choosing good over evil as with determining ourselves in all choices according to the good pleasure of God.

Mary, by the Holy Spirit, knew her nature was such that the imperative to obey God was freedom to act as her total nature dictated. Freedom for her was to be the person God made her to be. "Now this Lord is the Spirit and where the Spirit of the Lord is, there is freedom" (2 Co 3:17). The Spirit within her gave her a new, inner law that freed her from any formalized extrinsicism.

She received her holiness through a freedom that the Holy Spirit gave her in a continued growth process that was first radicated in His gift of faith. In this faith Mary assented to God's plan of salvation as taught in the Old Testament. She received in faith the new message of God that the Messiah was coming and she was to be His mother.

She responded in faith to the love of God by her complete surrender to serve Him in all things.

Her faith led her holiness to a strong hope that with God all things are possible. God could do whatever He wished with her. She would hope for a greater fulfillment of God's glory even though she already had experienced a great share in that glory.

But her holiness is measured and described in terms of love that in Mary grows out of the Spirit's faith and hope operating within her at each moment of her life. Mary was freed to love. She freely placed herself in service to God's Word, an inner presence of God's love incarnated and living in her. As she received in prayer experiences of God's love calling her to participate in a return of love, Mary became progressively more free to love others by seeking to serve them.

She experiences always the paradox that to be free is to become a slave to serve others in love. She knew that she was called to serve others in love.

> You were called, as you know, to liberty; but be careful, or this liberty will provide an opening for self-indulgence. Serve one another, rather, in works of love, since the whole of the Law is summarized in a single command: Love your neighbor as yourself (Ga 5:13-14).

Mary is holy, both because God has filled her with His Spirit of love and because she freely cooperated with His grace. We are privileged by that same Spirit to recognize her holiness as normative for all of us. If Mary, so holy by God's grace and her continued cooperation, why not we?

MARY OF NAZARETH

Mary knelt at Nazareth
And suddenly beneath her breath
Lay Jesus, and she loved Him;
Mary sang at Nazareth
And listened to the childhood breath
Of Jesus, and she loved Him, loved Him,
Then He grew and no one knew
The wonder of her son,
The years of waiting done,
He came to make all mankind one;
Mary wept at Nazareth
Remembering the dying breath of Jesus,
And she loved Him, loved Him,
Now the whole world's Nazareth
In every man she hears the breath
of Jesus, and she loves Him.

                              Bill Peffley

6

Mary — The Valiant Woman

Oscar Wilde once wrote: "There are times when Sorrow seems to be the only truth. Other things may be illusions of the eye or appetite, made to blind the one and cloy the other, but out of Sorrow have the worlds been built."

There is a certain wisdom that touches ultimacy which comes to us only through suffering. In such sufferings our hearts become purified of the cancerous illusions that make us think that we are the center of the universe, that we are God and we can control our lives. Reality, we mistakenly think, is only the way it appears to us. When we have pronounced our verdict on God, ourselves and others, on the world conditions, so be it because there is no other way!

But suffering *can* often be (it is not always) the occasion of God's Spirit creating in us a new heart,

> Sacrifice gives You no pleasure,
> were I to offer holocaust, You would not have it.
> My sacrifice is this broken spirit,
> You will not scorn this crushed and broken heart
>   (Ps 51:16-17).

St. Paul wrote a letter to the Corinthians that caused them great pain. But he used that occasion to teach them the possibility of suffering becoming a good if it leads to a conversion.

> . . .I am happy now—not because I made you suffer, but because your suffering led to your repentance. Yours has been a kind of suffering that God approves, and so you have come to no kind of harm from us. To suffer in God's way means changing for the better and leaves no regrets, but to suffer as the world knows suffering brings death. Just look at what suffering in God's way has brought you: what keenness, what explanations, what indignation, what alarm! (2 Co 7:9-11).

Suffering can give us the occasion for pushing ourselves to "see" what we failed to see before when our eyes were darkened by the spirit of the "natural" man. The Holy Spirit gives us a deepening vision to see inside of events and see there the loving hand of God bringing about greater good. "The inner man is renewed day by day. Yes, the troubles which are soon over, though they weigh little, train us for the carrying of a weight of eternal glory which is out of all proportion to them. And so we have no eyes for things that are visible, but only for things that are invisible; for visible things last only for a time and the invisible things are eternal" (2 Co 4:16-18).

We do not naturally like to suffer. Of ourselves we would never see any good in such and so we would, with the best of the worldlings, seek at all cost to avoid suffering. Like Moses in the desert before the burning bush, we need to be stripped of our securities as we fall down before the inscrutable, awesome Yahweh. In our weakness, God becomes our sole strength.

...the Lord said to me: 'My grace is enough for you; My power is at its best in weakness.' So I shall be very happy to make my weaknesses my special boast so that the power of Christ may stay over me and that is why I am quite content with my weaknesses and with insults, hardships, persecutions and the agonies I go through for Christ's sake. For it is when I am weak that I am strong (2 Co 12:9-10).

The early Christians had received the message of Jesus and had the Spirit's courage to live it. They were men "thought most miserable and yet we are always rejoicing; taken for paupers though we make others rich, for people having nothing though we have everything" (2 Co 6:10). Their Master suffered and He taught His followers how also to suffer:

Happy are those who are persecuted in the cause of right; theirs is the kingdom of heaven. Happy are you when people abuse you and persecute you and speak all kinds of calumny against you on My account. Rejoice and be glad, for your reward will be great in heaven; this is how they persecuted the prophets before you (Mt 5:10-12).

The joy of Jesus' Spirit would be given them in their sufferings. This joy would be grounded in the *hope* that out of these sufferings there would come a share in Christ's glory. He suffered, "obedient unto death, the death of the cross" (Ph 2:8) and for this reason He was glorified. So also His disciples are filled with courage "for the sake of the joy which was still in the future" (Heb 12:2).

COURAGE TO BE A CHRISTIAN

Such followers of Jesus are promised sufferings on the physical as well as on the psychic level, brought on by outside agents or from a force within themselves. But they would learn that the greatest sufferings would come in the interior, spiritual struggle to let Jesus Christ be total Lord in their lives. Man clings to things and thus seeks to find his identity through possessions. But Jesus comes into our lives and demands that we give up *all* in order to possess Him as our *ALL*.

> There is one thing you lack. Go and sell everything you own and give the money to the poor and you will have treasure in Heaven. Then come, follow Me (Mk 10:21).

As long as our following of Jesus is kept impersonal, on the level of observing the large, extrinsic commandments, it is easy to be a Christian. But when God begins to ask for a more total commitment of our whole life to serve Him, then things begin to get sticky. We squirm, resist, find excuses, rationalize ourselves and put off giving our complete "yes." In a word, like the rich young man, we turn away saddened because we are not ready to pay the price Jesus is asking. "His face fell at these words and he went away sad, for he was a man of great wealth" (Mk 10:22).

MARY COURAGEOUS

Mary will always be the model of all who wish to go the total way in following God's holy will. Men do heroic deeds in war, in overcoming the forces of nature. But there is a conquest of the human heart that requires the greatest courage. In this area, women have been outstanding in their sensitivity to God's demands and in their generous self-giving to God and neighbor. And Mary is the most *valiant* woman of them all for she surrendered herself totally. She allowed God to do with her whatever He wished.

She made her choice each moment of her life to allow God to be God in her life. "You shall love Yahweh your God with all your heart, with all your soul, with all your strength" (Dt 6:5). Her oblation in the Annunciation summed up, not a theological position, but the way she had lived all her life and the way she wanted to live her whole life: "I am the handmaid of the Lord; let what you have said be done to me" (Lk 1:38).

She had the courage to be sincere with God; therefore she, in her *Magnificat* could honestly call herself His *handmaid.* Mary lived the spirit of the Old Testament *Anawim* for she had deeply experienced that God had looked upon His *lowly* handmaid (Lk 1:48).

Her humility gave her strength over all enemies. With the courageous Judith she praised God's power in overcoming the enemies of her people Israel. Mary also could sing:

> I will sing a new song to my God.
> Lord, You are great, You are glorious,
> wonderfully strong, unconquerable.
> May Your whole creation serve You!
> For You spoke and things came into being,
> You sent Your breath and they were put together,
> and no one can resist Your voice (Jd 16:13-17).

Sinless Mary loved her people. She courageously could pray for Israel as Queen Esther did:

> As for me, give me courage,
> . . .save us by Your hand,

and come to my help, for I am alone
and have no one but You, Lord.
. . .Nor has Your handmaid found pleasure
from the day of her promotion until now
except in You, Lord God of Abraham.
O God, whose strength prevails over all,
listen to the voice of the desperate,
save us from the hand of the wicked,
and free me from my fear (Est 4:17r-17z).

When the angel gave her the message that she was highly favored to be the mother of the Messiah, the Son of the Most High, who was destined to rule over the House of Jacob and his reign would have no end, Mary courageously offered herself as the daughter of Sion that her people Israel would be restored to God's universal favor over all nations.

Her *Magnificat* is not original to her. Mary was deeply filled with the piety of her courageous ancestors Abraham, Isaac, Jacob, Rebecca, Judith, Esther, Ruth, Hannah, David. What is new is Mary's courage to live totally for God, centering her whole life around Jesus whom she was carrying to her cousin Elizabeth.

THE SWORD OF SORROW

She brought her treasure to the Temple to offer herself along with Him totally to God. He was all she would live for. Simeon, prompted by the Holy Spirit, recognized her in her poverty and reverence. He approached and took the Child Jesus from her arms. Here is the new Israel, "the glory of Your people Israel" (Lk 2:32).

Turning to Mary, Simeon spoke these words that foretold what the Valiant Woman would have to suffer because she wanted only to be God's handmaid:

> You see this child: he is destined for the fall and for the rising of many in Israel, destined to be a sign that is rejected—and a sword will pierce your own soul too—so that the secret thoughts of many may be laid bare (Lk 2:34-35).

Mary had marveled at the words that the angel Gabriel, Elizabeth, the shepherds and Magi, Simeon and Anna had spoken in praise of her son. She wanted not honors from men but only the honor to serve her God. Here Mary is being taught by the Holy Spirit. There is no serving Jesus Christ without suffering. Simeon foretold that her Son would be a sign of rejection. He would suffer, she *too* would have a sword of sorrow pierce her heart.

THE WOMAN OF THE DESERT

Mary's suffering would unfold in her submissive obedience to the will of God. There would be no one moment, not even at the foot of the Cross, that would satisfy this prophecy of Simeon. Mary becomes the Mother of Jesus Christ, not merely at Bethlehem, but more so in a progressive surrendering of herself in the darkness of faith, hope and love to serve her Lord. As she suffers with Christ, He becomes more fully born. His Body is the Church.

Mary's sufferings must be seen on a deeper level than what Christian meditation usually wrings out of meditating on her flight into Egypt, her seeking her lost Son in Jerusalem, her witnessing of Him dying on the Cross.

Perhaps St. John the Evangelist, to whom Jesus gave Mary as mother, can lead us into a new understanding of Mary, the Valiant Woman.

St. John knew Mary more intimately in that early Christian community than any other member, especially at the time he wrote his Book of Revelation. St. Luke had passed on to the Christians more details. Lesser minds sought to fill in the areas of Mary's earthly life not recorded in Holy Scripture with apocryphal writings. But John, in a masterly way, leads us to a higher understanding of Mary. Mary's greatness is an interior greatness brought about by Jesus' Spirit. He has made her great and only He can reveal to Christians Mary's true greatness.

When we go to the Johannine writings, especially the Gospel and the Book of Revelation, we open ourselves to the mystery of Mary that lies even beyond the historical details that the Synoptic writers offer us about Mary. We find Mary, the mother of Jesus, portrayed as involved in the history of salvation. In the Gospel scenes of Mary at Cana and at Calvary, she is addressed as "Woman," by her Son. She is intimately associated in both cases by Jesus in His redemptive work, far beyond her historical act of giving birth physically to Jesus.

We can best understand Mary's true valor and courage by going to John's portrayal of the *woman* in *Revelation*. Here we will understand Mary's heroic sufferings in a partnership of the redemptive sufferings of Christ. We will avoid seeing her sufferings separated from those of Christ. We will see how her sufferings make her the Valiant Woman even today in our regard.

Turning to the Book of Revelation we find Mary's true strength in the presence of cosmic sufferings portrayed in powerful symbols that continually yield deeper understanding as we listen to the Spirit teach us a true spiritual devotion to Mary.

> Now a great sign appeared in heaven: a woman, adorned with the sun, standing on the moon, and with the twelve stars on her head for a crown. She was pregnant and in labor, crying aloud in the pangs of childbirth. Then a second sign appeared in the sky, a huge red dragon which had seven heads and ten horns, and each of the seven heads crowned with a coronet. . . and the dragon stopped in front of the woman as she was having the child, so that he could eat it as soon as it was born from its mother. The woman brought a male child into the world, the son who was to rule all the nations with an iron scepter and the child was taken straight up to God and to His throne while the woman escaped into the desert, where God had made a place of safety ready for her to be looked after in the twelve hundred and sixty days.
>
> . . .As soon as the devil found himself thrown down to the earth, he sprang in pursuit of the woman, the mother of the male child, but she was given a huge pair of eagle's wings to fly away from the serpent into the desert, to the place where she was to be looked after for a year and twice a year and half a year. So the serpent vomited water from his mouth, like a river, after the woman, to sweep her away in the current, but the earth came to her rescue; it opened its mouth and swallowed the river thrown up by the dragon's jaws. Then the dragon was enraged with the woman and went away to make war on the rest of her children, that is all who obey God's commandments and bear witness for Jesus (Rv 12:1-17).

IN PANGS OF CHILDBIRTH

John portrays the woman in the desert as pregnant and in labor, *crying* out as she suffers to bring forth her

child. We can see, as commentators have pointed out,[1]
that John uses *woman* both in Rv 12:1 and in the Cana
and Calvary narratives in a typological sense that goes
beyond either Mary individually or the Church, yet that
embraces both at the same time. Mary is the prototype of
the Church because she is the mother of Jesus Christ.
Christ is in His Church as the Head to His Body. It is Mary
who gave birth to this one Christ who continues as the
same Christ in the Church. Mary, therefore, is the spiritual
mother of all the members of the Church. It is not by any
adoption in a symbolic way at the foot of the Cross when
she takes John, the beloved disciple, as her son that she is
our mother and, therefore, a true sign of our Mother the
Church, but solely because she is and always will be the
mother of Jesus Christ. We are her offspring because we
have been born by the same Spirit that fills Mary in the
Incarnation and fills the Church to make us brothers and
sisters of Christ, "to become true images of His Son, so
that His Son might be the eldest of many brothers"
(Rm 8:29).

Mary began her sufferings to bring forth her spiritual
offspring when Simeon foretold that a sword of sorrow
would pierce her heart (Lk 2:35). She was being called
into a more intimate role of suffering with her Son Jesus
who would be a sign of rejection for His people Israel.

"MY FATHER'S BUSINESS"

One of the greatest pains that a mother can experience is to realize that the life she gave to her child cannot
be possessed forever. Her maternal instincts tear her apart
the day her child makes her realize he is independent and

not her total possession. Mary grew in courage, not so much because she was asked by God to surrender her Son Jesus to God's plan that went against her natural desires, even though there was suffering on this account, but, more so because God was asking her, in faith, to have a greater role in co-suffering with Christ against the evil forces.

Mary suffered as she and Joseph sought the lost Child for three days, only to find Him in the Temple teaching the doctors of the Law.

> . . .and His mother said to Him: 'My child, why have you done this to us? See how worried your father and I have been looking for you.' 'Why were you looking for me?' He replied. 'Did you not know that I must be busy with My Father's affairs?' But they did not understand what He meant (Lk 2:48-50).

Mary did not understand. She is valiant not because she suffered but because in her sufferings she surrendered in faith and loving obedience to God's holy will. The sword continually pierced her in those relatively peaceful, joyful years at Nazareth because the Spirit constantly was preparing her for greater readiness and promptitude to say her "yes," to whatever awaited her in her relations with Jesus.

"MY HOUR HAS NOT COME YET"

At the wedding feast of Cana, Mary turns to Jesus and simply says: "They have no wine" (Jn 2:4). Jesus answers: "Woman, why turn to Me? My hour has not come yet." This could sound like a reprimand, another suffering as Mary is reminded that she is not to possess her Son who has come for something greater than merely to be her Son. Her true sufferings came in realizing through the Holy Spirit that Jesus was calling her to share in His "hour" when He would reach the peak of His earthly existence.

Jesus' use of the word *woman* in addressing Mary, although not uncommon in Semitic speech, must have stirred within Mary a new understanding that she was to be related to the Genesis prophecy when her seed would crush the head of the serpent.

> I will make you enemies of each other:
> you and the woman,
> your offspring and her offspring.
> It will crush your head
> and you will strike its heel (Gn 3:15).

When His hour would come and He would be raised up to draw all men to Himself (Jn 12:32), Mary would have a share in that hour. Jesus had come for this, to overcome the Prince of darkness. He was the Light struggling with the Powers of Darkness (Jn 1:9-10). "It was to undo all that the devil has done that the Son of God appeared" (1 Jn 3:8).

"WOMAN, THIS IS YOUR SON"

His hour came when He was raised aloft. It was His hour of complete emptiness in utter poverty of spirit and surrender to the will of the Father out of love for all of us. Yet it was also His hour of victory and triumph over the evil forces. He was "a light to enlighten the pagans and the glory of Your people Israel," as Simeon prophesied (Lk 2:32).

St. John, who stood beside Mary, sees Christ's triumphant victory in that moment of apparent defeat. He describes Calvary in the *Book of Revelation*:

> The great dragon, the primeval serpent, known as the devil or Satan, who had deceived all the world, was hurled down to the earth and his angels were hurled down with him. Then I heard a voice shout from heaven: 'Victory and power and empire forever have been won by our God and all authority for His Christ, now that the persecutor, who accused our brothers day and night before God, has been brought down. They have triumphed over him by the blood of the Lamb and by the witness of their martyrdom, because even in the face of death they would not cling to life. Let the heavens rejoice and all who live there' (Rv 12:9-12).

In that hour of utter darkness for Mary, when her heart was torn in two at the terrifying sight of her Son agonizing unto death, she too enters into a oneness of suffering with Jesus. The paradoxical law of life becomes fulfilled in her and in her Son: "Nothing lives but something must die. Nothing dies but something else lives." She had reached the peak of what the Church and we individually are called to be: co-sufferers with Christ filling up the Body of Christ (Col 1:24). The Valiant Woman had surrendered herself totally so that she lived only for God.

In the paschal mystery, she passes over with her Son from the holding on to her life to a complete giving, even unto the extreme pains of physical and spiritual dying. Mary experiences the prophecy of Isaiah: "The heart of each man fails him, they are terrified, pangs and pains seize them, they writhe like a woman in labor" (Is 13:7-8).

The greatest suffering and the greatest call to human courage is found in love. Mary is called by Christ to forget her final possession of her own life and even her holding to Jesus as her Son. Her "fiat" said at the Annunciation now reaches its full realization at the foot of the Cross.

Through her sufferings united with those of Christ, Mary is called "Woman" and she understands in a new way that she loses her Son in one way but gains Him in her new offspring.

> Then the dragon was enraged with the woman and went away to make war on the rest of her children, that is, all who obey God's commandments and bear witness for Jesus (Rv 12:17).

Mary does not become our spiritual mother at the foot of the Cross because Jesus merely entrusts her to St. John. She is our mother because she is the mother of Christ. Jesus Christ born of Mary and the same Jesus Christ on Calvary forming His Mystical Body of which we are His members form a unity. In Jesus we have our spiritual birth and existence as children of God. As Mary gave Him birth, therefore, she is also our mother. "Christ's words (on the Cross), far from creating the motherhood of grace, only presuppose it."[2]

Because Mary was courageous enough to allow God to possess her completely and do with her whatever He wished, she suffered with Christ. Yet this Valiant Woman in her pains is glorified in becoming the mother of an offspring, a new nation more numerous than the stars of the heaven, than the sands of the seashore.

> Yes, from this day forward all generations will call me blessed, for the Almighty has done great things for me (Lk 1:48).

A WOMAN SINGS

A virgin sang in the summer
soft was her song
soft as the rustle of grain
rich with the promise of grain.

A bride once sang in an autumn
happy her song
free as a leaf in the wind
sure as an oak in the wind.

A mother sang in the wintertime
tender her song
sweet with the feel of a child
warm with a love for a child.

A widow sang in the springtime
somber her song
sad as a hillside of stone
sad as a grave sealed in stone.

A woman sings through the seasons
sings through the grain
sings on the wind
sings in the stone
sings of her child
sings of a Son who had grown
a Son and a rolled-away stone.
She sings of a Son
and a song of a rolled-away stone!

Bill Peffley

7

Mary and the Church

One of the basic models or analogies found in devotion to Mary among Christians up to the time of the Protestant Reformation is that of Mary–Church. In using Mary as a prototype of the Church we must keep in mind the unity found in the plan of God. Mary is a reality in regard to the Holy Spirit who constantly comes upon her to bring forth Christ. A similar begetting of Jesus Christ through the power of the Holy Spirit is continuously being realized in the lives of individual Christians and in the Church as the collective membership in the Body of Christ.

In speaking of Mary and the Church we are helped by Ticonius of the third century whose fourth rule for interpretation of Holy Scripture, *de specie et genere*, had influenced so greatly the early Fathers, especially St. Augustine and his followers. The genus is hidden or concealed under the species, i.e. the whole body is represented by one member. When applied to the relation of the Church to Our Lady we see what is mentioned in the Gospels as applied to Mary is to be realized later and applied to the Church as from species to genus. The genus is concentrated in the species in anticipation, but always according to the design of God for the total salvation process of the human race. Thus what we can say about the Church in general can be applied to Mary in a unique, preeminent way. The same can be applied to the individual soul but in a singular way where the emphasis is put on the degree of perfection or imperfection and not on the uniqueness of the fullness of the perfection possessed.[1]

In venerating Mary as Mother of the Church, Christians throughout the centuries have struggled to balance off two extremes that would distort and correct thinking of Mary's position in the Church. On the one hand there has always been need not to put Mary outside of the Church. This is especially a danger when Mary's prerogative of having been preserved always from original sin is not correctly taught. For this reason the *Constitution on the Church* of Vatican II has stressed that Mary is a member of the Church, in need of redemption as all of us.[2]

The other danger is to make Mary a simple member like all of us. She is a member needing Christ's redemption, yet she is the first and most excellent member of the Church, higher in honor than all angels and all other human beings because she is related, not only in her physical motherhood[3] of Jesus Christ, but forever on a spiritual plane to the source of the Church, Jesus Christ, the Head, and the informing Holy Spirit that gives God's divine life of Jesus Christ both to Mary and to the Church. St. Augustine calls our attention to Mary's dignity in regard to us:

> Mary is clearly the mother of the members of Christ. . .since she cooperated out of love so that there might be born in the Church the faithful who are members of Christ their Head.[4]

The Heavenly Father sends and gives His only-begotten Son, made flesh by her conceiving through God's gift of the Holy Spirit who brings about the Incarnation. It is the Spirit that effects Mary's divine motherhood. Forever is Mary thus intrinsically related to the Person of the Blessed Trinity in a way that no other created being has ever been or ever will be related. It is impossible to think of Mary without thinking of her relationship to the Father who, without being sent, comes to her through the Father's sending of the Spirit. The Spirit is sent and given to Mary in order that the Son may be sent and given by the Father through Mary to the whole world.

MARY RESTORED TO THE CHURCH

The Fathers of Vatican II, moved by the Holy Spirit, restored Mary to the Church. Before the Council there had developed in various parts of the Catholic world a movement to declare as defined dogma that Mary is the Mediatrix of all graces and is Co-Redemptrix. No doubt a great deal of confused thinking came from not considering Mary in her role within the Church and her cooperation with the Holy Spirit. With more of a spiritual view toward the Church as the Bride of Christ the Fathers of Vatican II made the role of the Holy Spirit more central to the Church.

A RETURN TO THE EARLY FATHERS

From the time of Venerable Bede to the present, there have been those who have viewed Mary's many privileges along with her role in our redemption as a separate causality, outside of the Church. This analogy of Mary and the Church has been in the Church from earliest times. But the patristic perspective was always one of Mary and the Church essentially in the Christological order of the economy of salvation. The primary interest of the early Fathers in linking Mary with the Church and vice versa was always to highlight the plan of salvation, but seen from the designs of God. They viewed the redemption of the human race as an action descending from God through space and time. This process reaches its most decisive realization when the Blessed Virgin Mary conceived the Word become flesh. But there is a continuity in the process, according to the plan of God so that the Church carries on, fulfills, realizes the same mystery that Mary so perfectly fulfilled in effecting the hypostatic union. Mary and the Church are in an analogous way the same thing, but two different moments in the action of God descending down to mankind, to individual souls in order to bring about that which God has already brought about in Mary and to some extent in His Church.

Salvation as viewed by moderns who have lost this patristic perspective is viewed more often as an action on a purely satisfaction, propitiatory basis ascending from humanity back to God, the juridical concept of repaying a debt to a great banker up above. It will be most profitable for us to return to the Fathers and examine their fundamental concept of Mary and the Church analogy. The more we can recapture their viewpoint, the more we will replace the Blessed Virgin at the head of the receiving humanity and the more we will see Christ as the active agent sent from the Father from Heaven in order to draw us back to Him through the instrumentality of the Church.

This patristic view will also constitute the best rapprochement with the Orthodox and Protestants. By considering the Church less as a visible Society and more as the Mystical Body of Christ, as the Spouse of Christ and the Mother of the people of God, of the living faithful, we will present a Church that is more biblical and more in keeping with the early traditions of the Church. But to do this we must go to the Fathers and see how they viewed the Church precisely as the Mother and Spouse of Christ. This is another way of saying that Mary constituted for them the perfect type and model of the Church as Mother and Spouse of Christ.

After the Council of Ephesus (431) the Fathers, at least in the East, concentrated their attention on the Divine Motherhood of Mary and did not develop this analogy of Mary-Church any further. Actually, the essential seeds had been planted in the period before the first half of the fifth century. With the death of Ambrose, Augustine and Cyril of Alexandria, all before the middle of the fifth century, there was no real new evolution in theological content of this analogy. So we can be content to trace the development of this image from early Christianity until the Council of Ephesus.

The basic points of similarity center around the motherhood and virginity of the Church and of Mary. The Church gives birth to the members of Christ's Mystical Body through the sacraments and through the faith. It is a virgin through its unblemished faith, its tenacity to orthodoxy, its espousal to Christ through grace. We find the grounds for this predication in the biblical language of Christ as the New Adam and the Church as the New Eve. Mary has the same two qualities but realized in a different manner. She is corporeally the mother of Christ and physiologically was a virgin. Yet spiritually, too, in the designs of God, she plays the role of the New Eve, in restoring the human race to the pristine life of God in their souls through sanctifying grace.

In a language that shows a relaxed typological thought, the Fathers could move not only back and forth, speaking of both the Church and Mary at the same time, but could even apply the same type of maternity and virginity to the individual soul in which God is born through grace and through a virginal espousal to Christ where the "two will become as one flesh." We have already shown how Justin, Irenaeus and Tertullian saw the Church in Mary by a juxtaposition of Mary and Eve. For Justin, Mary, acting as God's partner, much as Eve acted as Adam's partner, but alas, for our spiritual destruction, was instrumental in making a pact of salvation between God and man. By freely cooperating, she became Eve's counterpart and the perfect image of the Church in working out the redemption of the human race with Christ in her receptive activity as spouse and mother.

Irenaeus assigns an active role to Mary in the recapitulation by Christ of the whole human race back to God's original plan as children of God. Tertullian linked up Eve-Mary-Church so that both Mary and the Church become the second new Eve. "It comes about that just as Christ was born of a Virgin, we also are spiritually reborn of a Virgin cleansed of all spots through Christ. This Virgin is the Church."[5]

Nearly all the Fathers of the Alexandrian school link Mary's role in redemption with that of the Church. Clement of Alexandria forcefully identifies Mary with the Church:

One single entity is the Virgin-Mother. But I like to call her the Church. This unique Mother had no milk because she was not a woman as such. She is a virgin and a mother at the same time. She is spotless and undefiled as a virgin. She is loving as a mother. She raises her children and feeds them with holy milk, the child-like Word.[6]

Didymus of Alexandria speaks of the spiritual birth of us in the baptismal font. The Church is our Mother through the conception of the Holy Spirit, yet the Church remains wholly a virgin.[7] We see that which is so evident among the Alexandrians, especially Origen, and later among the Cappadocians who were strongly influenced by the Alexandrian typology, the Church is spoken of in terms of the Blessed Virgin without actually uniting the two. Gregory of Nyssa makes an analogy between the birth of Christ from the Blessed Virgin and the regeneration brought about in the soul through the Holy Spirit.

For that which took place corporeally in the Immaculate Mary when the fullness of Divinity in Christ broke forth through the Virgin takes place also in every soul that lives spiritually as a virgin.[8]

SAINT AUGUSTINE

Augustine reaches, among all the Fathers, the summit in his use of this analogy. The Church for Augustine is at the same time the Spouse of Christ and the Body of Christ, the two forming one body. This spousal, physical identity with Christ is brought about by the human nature that

Christ historically received from the Holy Virgin.

> Our very Life descended down to us and took our Death and
> killed it through the abundance of His Life. He thundered out
> to us that we should return to Him into that secret dwelling
> from whence He had come to us, into the very first virginal
> womb where a human creature, mortal flesh, wedded Him so
> that he would not always remain mortal.[9]

He is telling us that we must reenter into the first virginal
womb in order that we might be made God as He was
made man. This virginal womb of Mary, where is it found,
if not in the Church? This is the key to understanding all
of Augustine's sermons on the Nativity: Mary is a virgin
and mother; the Church is a virgin and a mother.

> When I ask you, is Mary the Mother of Christ, is it not because
> she brought forth members of Christ? You, I say, are members
> of Christ. Who brought you forth? I hear the voice of your
> heart: Mother the Church.[10]

For Augustine this is not sheer rhetoric but is based
on a true identity. "According to the flesh our Head had
to be born of a Virgin through an extraordinary miracle, to
show that His members, according to the Spirit, were to
come forth from the virginal womb."[11]

Many authors have thought that at times Augustine
treated Mary and her maternity of Christ as something less
than the maternity of the Church or the maternity of an
individual soul in sanctifying grace. What does Augustine
mean in saying: "Mary was more blessed for having had
the gift of faith in Christ than for having conceived Him in
the flesh"?[12] We, too, can say that the mere physical

maternity did not sanctify Mary. Augustine distinguishes perhaps too sharply between the physical maternity and her divine maternity of Christ brought forth through grace. Sanctifying grace brought forth in the soul and divine maternity are the same for him. Thus the sanctifying grace in the souls of Christians and Mary's sanctifying divine maternity through faith and divine grace are the same. This life-giving principle of God's own life, present both in Mary and in the individual soul, is preferred by Augustine to the mere physical act of giving flesh to Christ. This physical act is not what made Mary the Mother of Christ, but rather it was through grace and her perfect faith that she brought forth His life within her.

Thus there exists for all of the early Fathers who are summarized in a very articulate manner by St. Augustine, a vital, intimate relationship between the hypostatic order and the order of grace, between the physical Christ and the mystical Christ. The main reason, as has been earlier said, that the Fathers could pass so easily from one order to the other, as is seen so clearly in their interchange of mutual attributes predicated equally of Mary and the Church, is their incorporation into the scheme of two terms: Mary and the Church. The third term is the divine plan behind all the persons and events that have been used instrumentally by God to effect one and only one thing: that God would descend to this earth and give us His own Life that we might be able to ascend to Him in an eternity as children loving their Heavenly Father. Thus in the mind of God, that is ever present to the Fathers, there is no dichotomy between the human and the divine element in Mary's conception of Christ and in the Church's conception of regenerated children of God.

GRACE – A SPOUSAL-MATERNAL ACTION

Grace, viewed in the Blessed Virgin Mary or in the Church's sacramental system or in the individual sanctified soul, is always a participation in the incarnational act of Mary which is at the same time both maternal and spousal. In receiving and accepting divine grace, an individual Christian becomes the mother of Christ in a limited sense. Mary is unique in her maternity insofar as she brought forth both physically and spiritually, through grace and her faith, the whole Christ. She becomes the perfect type of regenerated humanity, the Church, in attaining its supreme fruit, through the feminine, maternal act of receiving Divine Life through the Holy Spirit.

But also Mary is the perfect fulfillment of the Universal Church and of any given individual soul in particular insofar as she is the virgin spouse. Mary, as also the Church, is more than virgin; they are with Christ, one flesh, one spirit. The union of Mary and Christ and the Church and Christ is a real union but evidently in the spiritual, mystical order. The virgin-spouse Mary must be understood not only in the crudest sense, as mere absence of flesh relations with some man, but as an absolutely spiritual, mystical character of union of soul with God. Here we understand the phrase of St. Augustine that Mary first conceived in her soul before she conceived in her womb.

MEDIATION OF MARY AND THE CHURCH

From what has been said, we can understand the insight of the early Fathers in linking up Mary with the Church and seeing in both of them the source of universal mediation with Christ the Head. The Church is humanity saved, but it is also that which saves humanity. It is a mediator of salvation, associated with the one Savior Jesus Christ in bringing about the recapitulation of the whole created world back to the original plan of God. It is the Savior's representative, "the two shall be as one flesh," here on earth. So too Mary is the most perfect, the fullest way, the peak of redeemed humanity, but she is also united in the saving of that same humanity by being associated with the Savior as a type of the very same identical saving role exercised by the Church.

In summary of the position of the early Fathers we can say that the center of the history of salvation, of God's merciful invitation to us human beings to become His children by adoption, is not the historical Christ separated, along with His Divine Mother, from the total process of restoring humanity to its pristine image. The center of this economy of human salvation is the Whole Christ, imparting salvation to mankind. The Church is His Mystical Bride forming one Body with Him in receiving the fruits of His work, His pleroma of graces. The Church is also the Mystical Mother giving birth to individual souls through the imparting of divine grace. Mary is the perfect type of the Church because in her are fulfilled perfect motherhood and she is the perfect spouse of Christ. Mary is placed in the center of the economy of salvation, in the center of the Church whose essence is to receive, as a spouse, the fruits of Christ, and to give birth, as a mother, to the people of God.

THE CHURCH – CHRIST'S BRIDE

The early Fathers freely associate Mary with the Church but outside of the spousal-maternal analogy there is little theological explanation of how Mary relates to the Church. Taking their bold language and relating it to the language of Vatican Council II found in its *Constitution on the Church*, especially with a new opening to the role of the Holy Spirit both in Mary and in the Church's conception of the Word of God through their virginity and maternity, we can draw out a deeper meaning both in our devotion to Mary and the Church.

Relating the Holy Spirit to the Church more intimately than a Roman ecclesiology had done in the Tridentine perspective, we see the Church as one who responds to God's loving invitation. The Church has its beginnings with a person that, under the power of the Holy Spirit, is consciously surrendering to God's holy will in all things. Such a person seeks to serve God's Word, becoming conformed to the mind of Jesus Christ.

H. Urs von Balthasar sees Mary's surrender in faith, through the power of the Spirit, as the fundamental act of the Church as subject over and against Christ.

> Mary is that subjectivity, which in her feminine and receptive way, through the grace of God and the overshadowing of his Spirit, is enabled fully to correspond to the masculine subjectivity of Christ. In Mary the Church that springs from Christ finds its personal center and the complete working out of its ecclesial idea. Her loving and hoping faith, in her feminine openness for the divine God-man Groom, is coextensive with the masculine principle imbedded in the Church of office and sacrament.[13]

Thus Christians in their true devotion to Mary will be drawn to a devotion to the Holy Spirit. For Mary's Uniqueness as mother of God comes from her cooperation with the Holy Spirit in faith and loving obedience. It is the Holy Spirit that effects *Church* in Mary at the deepest level

of her conscious surrender of herself. He it is who opened
Mary in a total self-giving to Christ.

The same Holy Spirit effects *Church* in us to bring us
into an ever-increased consciousness of the centrality of
Jesus Christ as Lord in our lives. The Spirit within the
Holy Trinity effects the most intimate union between
Father and Son. But the Spirit also differentiates the
Father and the Son in being their unifying, loving force.
We are joined to Christ as members to our Head by the
Spirit. "There is one Body, one Spirit" (Ep 4:4). Yet the
Spirit gives us a sense of our unique individuality, capable
of a free act of surrender to Christ.

MARY THE PROTOTYPE

We have seen the patristic view of Mary-Church. The
early Fathers could move freely from Mary to individual
Christians to the Church because of their ability to think
in terms of type and exemplar. Heribert Mühlen, in his
development of a theology of the Holy Spirit, gives us an
insight that can be helpful in our attempt to understand
better Mary's role in the Church.

Mary is not a mediator in opposition to Christ's
mediation. Her saving influences in the Church "flow forth
from the superabundance of the merits of Christ, rest on
His mediation, depend entirely on it and draw all their
power from it. In no way do they impede the immediate
union of the faithful with Christ. Rather, they foster this
union."[14]

She is a mother to us in the order of grace because
she was predestined by God to be the Mother of God. The
Holy Spirit was operative in her life from the first moment

of her existence, even when she was incapable of human acts. This was due to the decree of Divine Providence that freely on God's part gave an absolute and irrevocable determination of Mary toward this function. And yet "in an utterly singular way she cooperated by her obedience, faith, hope and burning charity in the Savior's work of restoring supernatural life to souls. For this reason she is a mother to us in the order of grace."[15] She cooperated with the Spirit. She freely said her "yes." She truly suffered the harrowing martyrdom of her interior spirit on Calvary. How are these two reconciled—the predestination of Mary through God's free decree that gave her the overshadowing of the Holy Spirit, confirming her in grace to fulfill all that was to be asked of her in her role as mother of Christ, along with her free choice to cooperate?

Mary is not in the same sense the mother of the Church as she is the mother of Christ. Using Mühlen's term, we can say that Mary is given a "consecrating" grace that is unique and never given to any other human being in the Church's history.[16] She is given a role of being the *prototype* of what it means for us to be members in the Church. She is the first one to be redeemed through the merits of Jesus Christ, not only quantitatively but also qualitatively since grace in her reached such a perfect victory over sin that she was immaculately pure without sin from the very first moment of her existence as well as throughout her whole life.

MARY'S INTERCESSION

Not only is Mary the prototype of the Church's act of fruitful faith and therefore the "normative bridal subjec-

tivity of the Church,"[17] but also because she is qualitatively the perfect Christian par excellence, in reality she is
the most active member in the Body of Christ. In Mary,
both at Pentecost and in her glorious life in Heaven at this
time in our history, the Spirit is most present and working
in a preeminent degree to bring Christ to us members of
Christ and to all other human beings. Not only is Mary
prototypical and exemplary of what we must become by
imitating her faith, hope and love, but she is also actively
interceding for all of us that the Holy Spirit be poured out
abundantly upon us.

This aspect of the motherhood of Mary within the
Church of Christ is clearly described in the *Constitution on
the Church*:

> This maternity of Mary in the order of grace began with the
> consent which she gave in faith at the Annunciation and which
> she sustained without wavering beneath the cross. This
> maternity will last without interruption until the eternal
> fulfillment of all the elect. For, taken up to Heaven, she did
> not lay aside this saving role, but by her manifold acts of
> intercession continues to win for us gifts of eternal salvation.
> By her maternal charity, Mary cares for the brethren of her
> Son who still journey on earth surrounded by dangers and
> difficulties, until they are led to their happy father-
> land. . . .But, just as the priesthood of Christ is shared in
> various ways both by sacred ministers and by the faithful, and
> as the one goodness of God is in reality communicated
> diversely to His creatures, so also the unique mediation of the
> Redeemer does not exclude but rather gives rise among
> creatures to a manifold cooperation which is but a sharing in
> this unique source.[18]

Mary's mediation is never outside of the Holy Spirit
who has been given to her so abundantly in order to bring

forth the full Body of Christ. It can never detract from the unique mediation of Christ, "For there is one God and one Mediator between God and men, Himself man, Christ Jesus, who gave Himself a ransom for all" (1 Tm 2:5-6). In fact, since her mediation flows from the grace of the Holy Spirit within her, it can only add to the fulfilling of Christ's mediation.

As we increase in our understanding and love of the Holy Spirit, we will also grow in greater true love of Mary and the Church. We will understand the dynamics of God's love for us who, in a process of sending His Spirit upon the virgin of Nazareth, begins to form His Word that dwells among us. Mary, through the Spirit, did not bring forth only the physical Christ. That Christ, in dying, lives in His resurrectional presence. The Heavenly Father is continuously sending His Spirit of love upon us who in union with Mary and all the Saints virginally receive His impregnation of God's Word within us. Through that same Spirit we, with Mary, become the Mother of Christ as we bring Him forth and give Him to all whom we serve.

Truly only the Holy Spirit can reveal to us the mystery of how Mary and we individuals are the Church, for it is not so much a speculative doctrine but an *experience* of being "the handmaid of the Lord" through the overshadowing of God's Spirit of love.

8

Mary in Glory

You must have asked yourself many times: "What will I be like after I die?" It is not so much the thought of losing the richness in our twentieth-century lives that makes us today very deeply interested in the topic of death and the life to come. One factor that explains our curiosity about our eternal future in the life beyond is the personalism that pushes all of us toward deeper and more intense relationships in love toward others. We want to become individuals, freed from the preconditionings of our hereditary past, our education, our social conformism. So desperately do we want love and desire to give true love in return.

Amid so much empty materialism, gross eroticism, violent crimes and meaningless absurdities found in our present society, we are constantly being pushed toward what Paul Tillich called "the ultimate concern." We begin to ask ourselves questions like: "What does it mean to live? Why do I act? Is it in order to live? Then, why live? What is the test of a *good*, human life? After I die, what happens? Will I really go on living and in what shape or form?"

The questioning is the first step toward a new level of existence. Unless I become reflective about my life and its meaningful direction that I am capable of giving to it, I shall always be a "self" in the world, fragmented and pitted against the "others." I need reflection to move me to a larger vision of meaningfulness. Reflection or contemplation allows me to stand on a spiritual mountain and see the past, present, and to some degree, the future. I can descend then to the nitty-gritty, knock-about world and I know now something of where I am going and why I do things.

ONENESS WITH THE COSMOS

Science can help me understand intellectually, to a certain degree, that I am physically related to other material bodies. I need oxygen to breathe, water to drink, clothing to wear, food to eat. I am in a way *one* with the things I touch, taste, see, hear and smell. They have a vital role to play in making me *become me.* I grow into greater consciousness of my unique self through the material world.

We can easily see how God has created all material bodies to move in a series of transformations into higher forms of life. One lower form yields to a higher form and thus, in a way, becomes raised to that higher form. We can truly say that we are moving always from death to life, from one form of energy to another, from one state of being to a higher state.

St. Paul describes a cosmic interrelationship wherein we and the whole subhuman cosmos together "groan" in our "vanity," in the obstacles that hold us back from

higher growth in the Spirit of God. But he also holds out
the hope that we and the whole material world will be
brought through the birth pangs into a new and more
glorious life.

> The whole creation is eagerly waiting for God to reveal His
> sons. It was not for any fault on the part of creation that it
> was made unable to attain its purpose, it was made so by God;
> but creation still retains the hope of being freed, like us, from
> its slavery to decadence, to enjoy the same freedom and glory
> as the children of God. From the beginning till now the entire
> creation, as we know, has been groaning in one great act of
> giving birth; and not only creation, but all of us who possess
> the first-fruits of the Spirit, we too groan inwardly as we wait
> for our bodies to be set free (Rm 8:19-23).

For St. Paul, man's redemption and glorification were
intimately tied up with that of the world as a total unit. As
man's fall had cosmic repercussions, so too his glorification
into the "new man" would touch the cosmos. It too would
somehow share in the "new creation." The semitic mind
conceived man and the material world in which he lived as
a unit, a community of interrelated beings on march in a
linear process to their completion. The whole of creation,
therefore, moved together in the attainment of fulfillment
or destruction. In the final attainment of the end toward
which all creation was moving there would be two distinct
parts of Christ's victory that are even now *in via*, but only
in the *parousia* will be complete. All creation that is now
subject to "vanity," whose rule is corruption, will be
liberated and transformed into harmonious submission of
service according to the mind of God, contributing to the
full glory of God that comes only from all created beings
operating fully as God had intended. This will be the

cosmic act of deliverance from corruption. It is intimately bound up with the first part of Christ's victory in the *parousia*, that is, the deification of human beings into sons of God "by participation" (2 P 1:4).

CHRIST IN GLORY

Our hope in the resurrection of our bodies and through us also the material universe is rooted in Jesus Christ. We cannot imagine what our future life will be like. But because Jesus is risen and we already are a part of His risen Body, we too can even now live in the coming of the resurrection. He is "the first-fruits of all who have fallen asleep" (1 Co 15:20). As through His human body Christ as an integral part of humanity touched all men, so by the resurrection of His human body, the bodies of all human beings and the whole universe would be given the possibility to be reoriented to God. This reorientation would lead eventually to a full resurrection in the spirit.

Christ Risen is now able to give us His Spirit. The indwelling Spirit imparts to our souls the ontological life of God through the divinely uncreated energies, but He exerts His influence on our bodies as well.

> And if the Spirit of Him who raised Jesus from the dead is living in you, then He who raised Jesus from the dead will give life to your own mortal bodies through His Spirit living in you (Rm 8:11).

MARY GLORIFIED

Not only is Christ the New Creation, therefore, but also He calls all of us who are in Him to be participators of that newness of life (2 Co 5:17-18). We are in all things to grow up in Him who is the Head (Ep 4:15). We are living members of His Body (1 Co 12:27; Ep 4:16). Of all the living members in Christ, Mary is the one most filled with His life-giving Spirit. The fullness of God's grace in her has fashioned her into the highest realization of what is attainable to all of us.

When the Church wishes to speak of Mary's glory, it evidently is not drawing from historical evidence. Aware that it is the Virgin-Spouse of Christ, always, like Mary, full of grace and empowered by Christ to lead the children of God into Christ's life, the Church over the centuries reflects on Mary's greatness. Out of this prayerful reflection upon Mary as Mother of God, upon her complete self-surrender in faith and love to God's service, the Church comes into a greater clarity about Mary's glory. And in that applied revelation the Church teaches us, at least implicitly, what will be also our glory to come.

The history of this belief can be traced within the Church's prayerful reflection on Mary's glorification in Holy Scripture, apocryphal stories, homilies of the Church Fathers, liturgical hymns and prayers. Holy Scripture spells out the central teachings of Christianity as found in the Christian Bible. Tradition is the awareness of the Church in history of the meaning of these revealed truths as applied in a progressive clarification to answer the needs of Christians throughout the ages. Tradition can never contradict Scripture, but it can explicate what is found in general terms in the Bible.

The doctrine of Mary's assumption, body and soul, into glory is not explicitly found as a revealed teaching in Scripture. Yet the Church does find in Scripture types of Mary's assumption that, when added to the Church's living oral tradition, confirm the belief of the faithful in her assumption. St. Paul speaks of such typology when he writes: ". . .and it was written down to be a lesson for us who are living at the end of the age" (1 Co 10:11).

The Church's praying over Scripture finds two texts that touch in an analogical manner the assumption of Mary. We have already discussed these two passages in detail: Gn 3:15 and Rv 12:1-6, 13-17. In the first, the seed of the woman would crush the head of the serpent and strike its heel. Mary is the New Eve, bringing forth Christ, the New Adam, and both He and she would triumph over evil.

The second, from the *Book of Revelation*, shows us the woman clothed with the sun, standing on the moon, with twelve stars on her head for a crown. She is rescued from the pursuing devil by receiving a huge pair of eagle's wings to escape from the serpent into the desert.

APOCRYPHAL DETAILS

In the first four centuries of Christianity, little speculation was given to the role of Mary in the history of salvation. Bitter theological battles were being waged among Christian thinkers concerning the two natures of Jesus Christ and the divinity of the Holy Spirit. Only after the bloody persecutions ceased and the divinity of Jesus Christ against the Arian heresy was solemnly proclaimed in the ecumenical Councils of Nicea (325) and Constantinople (381) did the Church reflect on Mary's relationship to Jesus Christ. In the Council of Ephesus (331) she was declared to be the *Theotokos*, the Mother of God.

From this basic prerogative the Church progressively pondered Mary's dignity and further relationships to the other members of the Body of Christ, her Son. The assumption or glorification of Mary, body and soul, in Heaven was apparently a belief held by the Christian faithful and developed at first in popular, highly imaginative apocryphal stories rather than in detached, theological speculation. One implicit support of the doctrine of the assumption can be found in the general lack of desire or curiosity to obtain Mary's relics. Nowhere do we find any attempt even to look for her physical body.

St. John Damascene of the eighth century, in his homilies on the assumption of Mary quotes an earlier Euthymian History that discloses that in 451 the sepulcher of the Mother of God was discovered in Jerusalem. Emperor Marcian and Pulcheria asked Bishop Juvenal of Jerusalem to send the coffin with her body to Constantinople. He replied that the coffin, not her body, was in Jerusalem. Apparently the Apostles had opened the tomb on the third day after her death and found only her burial garments.

The details of these apocryphal stories, often excessive in literary taste, are not important. The Church Fathers, such as Sts. Epiphanius, Modestus, Germanos, Andrew of Crete and John Damascene, in their homilies usually presented details gathered from such apocryphal writings, but gradually moved the consciousness of the faithful to a theological understanding of why God glorified Mary.

The argument given by the Greek homilists is one of convenience as in these words of St. John Damascene:

> Is it possible that the Source of Life, the Mother of my Lord, has died? It was fitting that what was composed of earth should again return to the earth and so be transferred to

Heaven, taking up from the earth the all-pure life which was given it in the deposition of the body. It was fitting that after the flesh had cast off the earthly and darksome weight of mortality in death, like gold in a furnace, it should come forth from the tomb incorruptible and pure, shining with the light of incorruptibility.[1]

Perhaps the most influential supporters of Mary's assumption into Heaven were the hymn-writers in the seventh to ninth centuries, such as John Damascene, Cosmas of Maiouma and Theophanus Graptos. Thousands of hymns were written affirming Mary's glorious transition to Heaven.

THE ASSUMPTION IN LITURGY

Until Emperor Justinian in the middle of the sixth century, there were no feasts celebrated to honor Mary. There was a primitive day to commemorate Mary as there was for the other saints and martyrs. This memorial celebration eventually became the feast of the Dormition or Assumption of the Virgin Mary. It was soon celebrated all over the East by the end of the sixth century. The Eastern Churches celebrated other feasts of Mary, such as her Conception, Nativity, Presentation in the Temple, the Annunciation, but the Assumption was the central feast of Mary. By the thirteenth century it was preceded by several weeks of Lent-like fasting. All of these feasts were gradually introduced into the Roman Church from the East.

Louis Bouyer writes: "If the cult of the Blessed Virgin Mary occupies a considerable place in the Western Catholic Church, one could say that in the East it has completely overrun the Liturgy."[2]

The Eastern liturgical prayers, hymns and homilies show that this doctrine of Mary's assumption into Heaven was not dry theological speculation but an intuition of the faithful who, in prayer over centuries, began to realize Mary's glorification. They professed that Mary, the Mother of God, has been raised incorruptible, body and soul, the total person of Mary, and is now in glory in Heaven.

Typical of such hymns is the one sung in the Liturgy in honor of Mary, Mother of God, for the feast of the Assumption:

> In thee, O spotless Maiden,
>> The bounds of nature are overstepped:
> Childbearing is virginal;
>> Death is but a pledge of life.
> After giving birth, thou art a maiden,
>> After death, alive.
> O Godbearer,
>> Thou dost save us, thy heritage,
> Unceasingly!

But such hymns and prayers also highlight and concretize a basic Christian revelation. Matter is not evil, but is one with man's spirit. The total human person is divinized by God's Spirit to enter into eternal glory.

MARY'S GLORY – OUR HOPE

We see that the faithful of both Christian East and West had a conscious belief that God glorified Mary upon her death. Although this has been for Catholics declared a dogma by Pope Pius XII on November 1, 1950, it has its force because it has been a truth believed and taught in the Church for many centuries.

What we Christians believe God has done to Mary, we also firmly believe God will do to us if we die in the Lord. We believe that our whole person, body and soul, will be raised to a new level of existence. God created us to be *"whole"* persons. The whole person, the biblical physical, body-man, *soma* in Greek, in death does not experience a separation of body and soul. There is an end to our immersion in a lower stage of our evolutionary development.

We believe in the mystery of Mary's assumption and as we celebrate her glory, we profess that we too will enter into a body-soul-spirit resurrection. I believe that this teaching of Mary's glorification says much about other human beings, even now sharing somewhat in her glory.

THE HEAVENLY CHURCH

It has already been noted that for centuries Catholic devotion to Mary stressed her in isolation, often even from Christ, mostly as separated from the rest of the Church of which she is the prototype. The dogmatic definition of her assumption brought an end to such a faulty accent.[3] Pope Pius XII's Apostolic Constitution, *Munificentissimus Deus*, (November 1, 1950), expressed the hope "that faith in the bodily assumption of Mary into Heaven may make our faith in our resurrection both stronger and more active." But there was no understanding that Mary was a model of our own individual glorification and that of the Heavenly Church.

This evolved in the writings of theology immediately after 1950. These writings prepared for the enlightened document, *Lumen Gentium*, of Vatican II. This Constitution on the Church linked Mary in glory with the Church in glory.

The mother of Jesus, in the glory which she possesses body and soul in Heaven is the image and beginning of the Church as it is to be perfected in the world to come.[4]

If Mary is, therefore, the image and beginning of the Church, is it not possible to believe that as she is now in glory, so in a similar way are the saints who with her form the Heavenly Church? She is the most excellent member of the glorified Body of Christ. But she is a part of that communion or fellowship (*koinonia*, as the Byzantine Liturgy expresses it) of the Holy Spirit. It is the whole Heavenly Church that is glorified by Jesus Christ's Spirit and is the prototype of what all of us who make up the earthly Church will be in the future when we too will pass as Mary and the other saints through death passed into glory.

The glory of Mary and the glory of the saints is the glory of the Body of Christ, the Heavenly Jerusalem, the new creation. The Heavenly Church is no longer in pilgrimage but is in glory, and Mary is the holiest of all the members of that glorified Body of Christ. We stretch out in hope to reach also the state of glory that they enjoy. The Woman clothed with the sun is both Mary and the Heavenly Church. "The great sign is Mary as the Church."[5]

THE GLORY OF MARY IS OUR HOPE

What we believe God's Spirit has accomplished in Mary and in the other members of the Heavenly Church, we eagerly await to be accomplished in us. Our hope through Christ's revelation is that not only our soul, but our body, our total person, will be joined to the resurrectional life of the living Savior. But if our material being will reach its completion by a transformation and "ascension" from this earthly existence to an "incorruptible" one, the Christian faith expresses the hope that the whole cosmos will be transfigured into a "new creation." It is the glorified Christ that associates Himself as mediator in bringing the universe to its appointed completion "in order that God may be everything to everyone and everything" (1 Co 15:28). God's will is "to gather all creation both in heaven and on earth under one head, Christ" (Ep 1:10). Christ has complete primacy and dominion over the cosmic universe through His death and resurrection.

Mary, our Heavenly Mother, and the other saints, our glorified brothers and sisters, make it possible for us to hope for a share of their glory when we, by God's grace, will also become a part with them of the Heavenly Church, the Body of Christ in full glory. Then we will understand the prophetic words of St. Paul:

> May the God of our Lord Jesus Christ, the Father of glory, give you a spirit of wisdom and perception of what is revealed, to bring you to full knowledge of Him. May He enlighten the eyes of Your mind, so that you can see what hope His call holds for you, what rich glories He has promised the saints will inherit and how infinitely great is the power that He has exercised for us believers. This you can tell from the strength of His power at work in Christ, when He used it to raise Him from the dead and to make Him sit at His right hand, in heaven, far above every Sovereignty, Authority, Power or Domination or any other name that can be named, not only in this age but also in the age to come. He has put all things under His feet, and made Him, as the ruler of everything, the head of the Church, which is His body, the fullness of Him who fills the whole creation (Ep 1:17-23).

9

Mary, Pray for Us Now

There is only one goal that we hungrily seek after in all our aspirations, in all our thoughts and actions. We desire love—to be loved—which means necessarily to give love. Love is circular. In our human love, one seeks to give himself to the other. In so doing, he intuitively knows that he will expand in being his true self. He lets go of his self-containment and in an act of faith and hope, he seeks to serve the godly beauty in the one he loves. The other receives the gift of the lover. But then the roles are reversed. The receiver returns the gift by a self-surrendering "yes" while the one who first offered himself as a loving gift now joyfully receives the returned gift.

Love is man's most creative action for he touches the divine, both in himself and in the beloved. It is a haunting drive. We can even say it is the very uncreated energies of God loving in us, urging us to go beyond the limited and temporal, the spatial and perishable, to make union with the infinite. The miraculous power of love is that it makes us forget our own limits and creates in us a desire to be immortal. The urging of God within us when we love others is a stirring toward eternal life.

Yet true love can never think of one's own static, isolated perfection. True love that God is, as St. John describes in 1 Jn 4:7-21, is a humble service, an emptying, a losing of one's life to find it in the union attained with the beloved. St. Paul beautifully links up this losing of Christ's own life, His divinity, with even His *Kenosis* or emptying Himself even of His humanity, "obedient unto death, the death of the Cross" (Ph 2:8), so that out of the dying for us, Jesus Christ enters into His glory.

Jesus is the love of God for us acted out in the human language that alone convinces beyond any doubt—suffering unto death.

> God's love for us was revealed
> when God sent into the world His only Son
> so that we could have life through Him;
> this is the love I mean:
> not our love for God
> but God's love for us when He sent His Son
> to be the sacrifice that takes our sins away (1 Jn 4:9-10).

He offered Himself up in our place as a "sacrifice to God" out of love for us (Ep 5:2; Ga 2:20). Jesus Christ is He who loves us (Rv 1:5). Yet He lives now in glory, loving us and calling us into immortality. He lives in glory, loving us infinitely and interceding on our behalf that through His Spirit we may experience the eternal love of the Father. ". . .His power to save is utterly certain, since He is living forever to intercede for all who come to God through Him" (Heb 7:25).

Jesus is now in glory and lives to surround us with His healing love. This is the Good News that the Apostles preached: "You did not see Him, yet you love Him; and still without seeing Him, you are already filled with a joy so glorious that it cannot be described, because you believe" (1 P 1:8). Jesus died but lives in a new way, never to be separated from us. His glorious, triumphant presence transcends all space and time. Through His Spirit we can, in every place and at all times, receive His infinite, personal love for us individually.

The same Jesus of Nazareth lives in you and me. No one can separate Him from us. What He said and did, especially dying for me individually, He is always *now* doing. I walk in His presence. I am regenerated constantly by His love for me.

"COME TO ME"

He had said before He died that He would draw all men to Himself. "I shall return to take you with Me; so that where I am you may be too" (Jn 14:3). Of all the members of Christ's Body, who but Mary enjoys the highest glory and oneness with Jesus Christ? We have already seen the Church's belief over so many centuries in Mary's con-glorification, body and soul, with Christ. As she intimately shared in the life, suffering and death of her Son, so the Church believes Mary shares now in His glory (Rm 8:17). She had come to serve Him with the total surrender of herself. She also has come into glory with Him (Mt 25:34). Jesus is the "first fruits and then, after the coming of Christ, those who belong to Him" (1 Co 15:23). Mary belongs most intimately to Jesus as mother to Son, as the living member of His Body closest in relation to Him, the Head.

INTERCESSION OF MARY

Mary's glory, like that of Christ, is not a static enjoyment of a heavenly reward. Her glory consists in being present to Jesus Christ and through Him present to the Heavenly Father by the overshadowing of the Holy Spirit. But being present in love to her Son is to have His very own mind. It is to receive His infinite, perfect gift of Himself, but it is also for Mary to want continually to surrender herself in loving service.

As Jesus is now interceding for us, so Mary is united with Him in seeking to help us. If Mary on earth lived only for Christ, how much more now does Mary want to bring all beings to Him. The Church teaches us that Mary and all the saints who have died in the friendship of Christ are now living in glory. It means that Mary is, therefore, living with full consciousness, memory and understanding of our needs. She exercises acts of love and compassion towards all of us still in this earthly exile.

Can we believe that Mary, who loved Jesus Christ so ardently in her lifetime, does not now burn with love and zeal to share her Son with all of us? If St. Paul yearned with great zeal to become all things to all men in order to win them for Christ (1 Co 9:22), we can imagine without any exaggeration the interest and zeal of Mary in regard to all human beings. St. Paul felt a spiritual maternity toward those whom he formed. "I must go through the pain of giving birth to you all over again, until Christ is formed in you" (Ga 4:19). Mary, who in her earthly life gave birth to Christ, wants continually in her glory to form Christ in all the children He has given her.

We have seen Mary as a prototype of the Church, the collective Mother, the womb wherein all of us, redeemed

children of the Heavenly Father, are brought forth unto
Christ's new life. We must center here in a special way on
Mary as person, historically the mother of Jesus, and in
glory now vitally concerned with and lovingly relating to
us as individuals. We cannot, however, separate Mary's
loving activity on our behalf from her total submission to
Christ's unique intercession.

COMMUNION OF SAINTS

The Church has always taught doctrinally and devo-
tionally in the cult to the saints that there is communication between the living in this life and those living in
Christ in the life after death. Vatican II's *Constitution on
the Church* reiterates this constant tradition: "The Church
too has devoutly implored the aid of their intercession."[1]
We implore their intercession because we believe they are,
after death, even more alive and more loving, hence, more
desirous to help us than when they lived their earthly life.
Blessed Robert Southwell, an English Jesuit martyr of the
16th century, put it succinctly:

> Not where I breathe do I live,
> but where I love.

Those who die are as real as the love relationships
formed in this life. Their limitations and degree of reality
enjoyed by them are fashioned not by a material locali-
zation but by God's power of love within them. Faith
among Christians down through the centuries insures them
and us that we can be in spiritual communion with the
angels and saints, our loved ones, relatives and friends who
have passed through death into eternal life.

Among all Christians departed into life eternal, Mary is the most "possessed" by God's Spirit of love. She is "higher in honor than the Cherubim and more glorious beyond compare than the Seraphim" as the Byzantine Liturgy of St. John Chrysostom hymns her. She is more present to all of us than our most beloved parents, husband or wife or friends departed.

She is present to us by the immense "oneness" that she enjoys with the "oneness" of the Trinity. The prayer of Jesus to His Father in the Last Supper Discourse was fulfilled for His Mother, at least.

> Father, may they be one in Us,
> As You are in Me and I am in You, . . .
> with Me in them and You in Me,
> may they be so completely one. . .
> I want those You have given Me
> to be with Me where I am
> so that they may always see the glory
> You have given me. . .(Jn 17:21-24).

But Mary is also present universally to every human being by her activating love that seeks to serve the neediest of the children whom she ardently wishes to bring forth into God's life. Love of God in Mary is the uncreated energies of God seeking to become realized love through the humble service of Mary. At the heart of Mary's love and our love is a desire to share abundantly of the goodness God has given to us with others who do not have what we have.

The greater the gifts of love we receive, the more we have to share with others. Upon entering into her glory in Heaven, Mary was full of grace. She was already declared full of grace by the Angel Gabriel when the Holy Spirit overshadowed her and she surrendered completely to serve her Lord in her humble lowliness (Lk 1:38). Yet she grew in love of God as she allowed God's love in her to make her more open, more present, more serving to all who needed her. How she must have grown in grace as she served her Son Jesus at Nazareth for 30 years. At the foot of the Cross, how that grace must have reached a fullness that pained her to want to be present to each person in the whole world in order that the blood of her Son and God might not be poured out in vain.

GROWTH IN GRACE

Now, after 2,000 years (in our earthly reckoning) of serving the universe of human beings from her state of glory, how she has grown in greater grace, in greater love-presence of God-in-her toward the whole world. In a way, Mary needs us, all of us. Like a mother who needs a sick or retarded child to allow her the occasion and the conflict necessary for her to grow in greater self-giving love, so Mary needs the sinful and ignorant who live in darkness and absence of her Son. She lovingly intercedes for them as only a suffering mother can: "Father, forgive them, they do not know what they are doing" (Lk 23:34). She needs also the advanced contemplative to share her contemplative riches. The simple, ordinary Christian calls out a unique form of Mary's service as she seeks to urge him to greater generosity and intimacy with her Son. Thus Mary grows in greater love by exercising a loving service to her children.

Mary in glory is constantly concerned with God's children. Beginning in her earthly life, especially, as we pointed out earlier, at the foot of the Cross when Jesus gave John to her as her son and at Pentecost where she was at the center of the first Christian community interceding for the outpouring of the Holy Spirit, Mary progressively grew in greater understanding of her motherly concern for all human beings. God infused into her in a growth process, both in her earthly life and in her present glorified existence a greater knowledge of the needs of all human beings individually and gave her a love that could take each person as her child and minister the healing power of her Son.

Mary sees us all in God and loves us with the love that Jesus has for us. Through God's grace, she is able so completely to be at one with her Son that His understanding and love for us become also hers. She sees in each of us a part of herself because she sees us as a part, actually or potentially, of His Mystical Body. She wants only what Jesus wants for us. Her intercession, therefore, far from being separated from that of her Son, is one with His. As His intercession before His Father's throne is omnipotent, so Mary's intercession, one with Christ's, approaches to that degree of omnipotence. Her intercession is not of her own. It is of a similar nature as her words to the servants at the wedding feast of Cana: "Do whatever He tells you" (Jn 2:5).

MARY COMPASSIONATE

If Mary is in touch with all human beings and sensitive to their needs, how can we reconcile her being in the state of glory and still able to suffer with us? How do our coldnesses and tepidity affect her in glory? Mary has brought into glory not only her body, but also all of her experiences in human living. She can now re-live her suffering moments by expressing at will the experience once had but now applied to new experiences of relating to different events and persons from the initial experience.

As she has been in intimate and involving concern with human beings for almost 2,000 years, she has been in touch with each period of history in general and with the specific history of each person she has sought to help.

Such active concern brings her to this present moment, allowing her to compassionate and suffer where we fail to live as we ought. Our sinfulness must cause her sorrow, just as our cooperation with grace must add to her joy in Heaven.

APPARITIONS OF MARY

This might aid us in understanding how Mary can externalize her invisible presence and manifest a state of sorrow at the failings of God's children. Apparitions of Mary to individual Christians throughout the centuries can legitimately have a prophetic or charismatic role to play within the Church. We must always distinguish between public and private revelations. Anything touching upon essential doctrines and moral values comes under the competence and duty of the hierarchical magisterium in the Church. Apparitions of Mary or even of Christ or saints and angels to individuals are peripheral to elements essential to man's salvation and, therefore, are secondary. This is not to say such are not helpful.

Apparitions can call individual Christians who receive them or others who heed the messages given in such visions to a very concrete way of understanding important elements already clearly revealed and taught as a part of the Church's public revelation received from Christ and His Apostles. Mary, appearing at Lourdes, LaSalette or Fatima, can be exercising in a loving, maternal way her concern for her children in a given part of the world at a specific time in history.

E. Schillebeeckx gives us important norms to situate Marian apparitions within the larger context of God's salvation history.[2] 1. Such extraordinary, charismatic elements must be subordinate to the normal moral and religious life of grace informed by dogma. Such apparitions are never sources of new doctrines, but their message can stir people to new fervor and a return to the Church's traditional teachings and sacramental means of sanctification.

2. We do not have to accept apparitions with any divine faith since they are always secondary to the supernatural, revealed truths. It is always a question of our natural acceptance or rejection of them.

3. When the Church gives any approbation, this must not be construed as an infallible proof for the historical truth and authenticity of the apparition in question. No one is obliged to accept such authenticity. 4. The Church may bless shrines, establish liturgical feasts and popular devotions but again, such approbation does not pass any judgment on the historical authenticity.

MARY'S CONCERN FOR US

We can imagine Mary, the mother of Jesus Christ and of His many brothers and sisters, being especially concerned with the billions and billions of people, who through no fault of their own, never came to know that her Son is the Savior sent to enlighten the hearts of all mankind. God could touch their lives in any way He wished. But He has worked through the community called the Church. This Church owes its existence to Mary's first mothering of Jesus her Son. If people are shaped by a society so as not to know Jesus Christ as their Lord, then God uses His new creation, the society of His chosen people, whose mother is Mary, to touch them through their intercession and their direct communication with them in the life to come.

Man dies and brings into eternity that level of consciousness as a human being that he has reached throughout his human existence by making choices in accordance with his conscience. If the Church's doctrine about Purgatory has truth to it, it would seem that a therapy is at work in the life to come for those who have not totally separated themselves from God. As in this life, we are helped through the prayerful intercession of holy persons and their personal example acting upon our lives, so we can believe that the saints, especially Mary, will be used by God as channels of His healing for such as those who have not met Jesus Christ as their personal Lord and Savior.

It is this powerful intercession in Heaven of the saints that St. John writes about:

A large quantity of incense was given the angel to offer with the prayers of all the saints on the golden altar that stood in front of the throne; and so from the angel's hand the smoke of the incense went up in the presence of God and with it the prayers of the saints (Rv 8:3-4).

Mary and the saints are living members of Christ's Mystical Body. Love of God and neighbor never comes to an end (1 Co 13:8). We can never imagine that Mary and the other living members of Christ are "up there" in Heaven separated from us. They are where Christ is and Christ is present on earth growing in His members. His Body is growing both in Heaven and on earth. St. Paul understood well this interaction between the healthy members and the injured or needy members: "If one part is hurt, all parts are hurt with it. If one part is given special honor, all parts enjoy it" (1 Co 12:26).

Mary is truly in touch with us and eager to do all in order that Jesus become Lord and Master in our lives. "For He must be King until He has put all His enemies under His feet and the last of the enemies to be destroyed is death, for everything is to be put under His feet" (1 Co 15:26). Our lives will change if we can live in the active faith that assures us that Mary, the Saints, all of our departed loved ones are in intimate communication with us. The more we are united consciously to Christ, the more we are united to His living members. The closer the saints are united with the Head, Jesus Christ, the more they desire to help us.

And Mary is the one human being who is the closest member to Christ in His Body. True love of Christ's Spirit in her is constantly transforming her into an active, loving Mother of us individually. Many of us have had a childhood devotion to Mary that made her very present to us. Becoming religiously "educated," we have lost this living, childlike communication in love with her. We have all too often relegated our devotion to Mary, as in reciting the Rosary, to a moralistic meditation on her earthly mysteries in order to find an extrinsic model upon which to pattern our concrete living. Cannot our devotion to

Mary only too often be satirized as: "See Mary; see Mary run; run like Mary." We were taught never to do anything at a dance or on a date that Mary would not have done! That we have lost such a devotion can only be unto God's glory.

A NEW DEVOTION TO MARY

We express our devotion to Mary always in language that comes out of a definite culture. Today we are completely turned off in reading some of the expressions of St. Louis Grignon de Montfort such as "becoming Mary's slaves." He, no doubt, had a tremendous love for Mary and expressed that devotion in terms that were meaningful for him and his contemporaries of times past.

We have had to stand back in our devotion to Mary to examine what is essential from what is cultural, accidental, and perhaps in need of change. Both through a biblical revival and scholarly patristic research we have been brought to a new awareness of what is essential in true Christian devotion to Mary. Our insights through in-depth psychology and sociology, personalism in community relationships allow us to be more open to experience Mary both as an archetype of the virgin-mother that she was in the Incarnation, of what the Church is called always to be and what we, as individual Christians, have been destined in our Baptism to become.

Yet precisely because Mary is an historical person who lived as recorded in the Gospel as the Mother of Jesus and who the Church proclaims throughout 2,000 years of belief is glorified in body and soul, a sign of what awaits us, she is not only our archetype but she continues to be our Heavenly Mother.

It is only the Holy Spirit that Jesus releases from the depths of our hearts who can lead us into the presence of Mary as our Heavenly Mother. He can give us a true and growing experience of her loving care for us without taking away from the centrality of Jesus Christ's mediation. On the contrary, the Spirit teaches us that Mary's sanctity is the gift of God's grace that has ever rendered her the lowly handmaid seeking only to exalt her Lord and Savior. She is completely dependent on God's Word. She defines her greatness and her relationship to us solely in terms of loving service to Jesus Christ.

That same Spirit gives her and us the intuitive knowledge that she is always the Mother of God, full of grace, seeking through her powerful union with her Son to bring us forth as living children through His Holy Spirit.

MARY NOT THE CHURCH

Because Mary is an individual person and not a mere type of the Church collectivity, we can be devoted to her, person-to-person, in a way that we cannot be devoted to Mother Church. The Church is like Mary a Virgin and a Mother. Yet it enjoys a mission of teaching, sanctifying, administering through the extension of Christ's mission on this earth in time.

In this teaching, sacramental and pastoral ministry, Mary has not been confided a direct role. Through the Church, Christ lives and acts in space and time on this earth. Mary while on earth was not given a part in the Church's teaching, sacramental worship and priestly hierarchy.

Yet these functions of the Church, if they are to bring forth Christ's life effectively into our world today, must be rooted in grace, love and prayer. The Church is first Mary, feminine, contemplative, completely surrendered to the overshadowing of the Holy Spirit. Out of this obedient submission, the Church takes on the masculinity of Jesus Christ who ministered to the poor and the sick, the possessed and the sinful.

But we who are the church become one with Mary in our devotion to her in our life of prayer. Without deep prayer, we will always look upon Mary as an object, someone who aggressively in a powerful way obtains things for us. Such a devotion will always be a mockery and an offense to the Holy Spirit.

But as we stand before her icons and statues in our homes, churches or wayside chapels, the Holy Spirit will render us one with Mary. We will become devoted to her by not imitating her *actions* but by becoming what she is: the Virgin-Mother of God.

A few years ago, I was able to spend a semester at Tantur, the ecumenical institute for advanced theological research. It is located outside of Jerusalem on a knoll overlooking the fields of Bethlehem. The town of Bethlehem is about two miles away so often I enjoyed walking through the fields on its outskirts. The hills are dotted by numerous caves. My favorite occupation on such walks was to enter into these caves and go through a meditation.

It would begin by watching St. Joseph take Mary down from the donkey after their fatiguing journey. He enters the cave and leads Mary inside. As he places the lantern on a rock, Mary's eyes adjust to the dimness around her. There is a dankness, a wetness that makes it a bit difficult to breathe. She sees the mildewed straw, bugs, and insects scurrying about; the animals stand mute in their caked-dung. Cob-webs hang menacingly from the ceiling and walls. And then I always hear her say as she looks upwards: "God, you got to be kidding! Do you really want me to bring forth Your Son in this cave?" And God comes back with a sense of humor that only He can afford to entertain in such circumstances: "Yes, Mary, right on! Right on this dirty, stinky straw."

My Lord and my God! I fade in the background with the shepherds and the animals. Mary has brought forth God and laid Him in a manger. The cave is transformed into the most beautiful cathedral. It isn't architecture that makes the temple of God but *presence*! She has brought forth the presence of God into this broken segment of our world. The Body of Christ begins to grow and Mary is its Mother.

Mary is still that mediating presence of God in the caves of our hearts, in our broken, dark selves. It is His presence that can transform our caves into beautiful temples of God. But Mary is always there asking her Lord: "Do you really want me to bring forth Your Son in this cave?"

It's only a meditation, yet somehow it makes Mary seem more really the Mother of my Lord. I don't understand all the theological distinctions of her causality. All I know is that she is God's Mother and God continues to want her to bring Jesus Christ forth within me, in my daily life. I know also she is my mother and I love her for the great love she has for me. I always leave the Bethlehem cave knowing that God is a presence of love that can transform the dank darkness in my heart into the warmth and light of the Spirit of Jesus. And I know also that Mary is a similar presence of love as she lovingly mediates the presence of her Son for me in my life.

As we pray "Holy Mary, Mother of God, pray for us *now...*," we will experience her loving, motherly presence. She will become the channel of grace that will make us true members of the Church, of Christ's Body. We will live constantly in her holy presence, trusting that she who is all powerful before her Son will intercede for us, not to obtain so much this or that favor, but more importantly that we become like her, a living oneness with Jesus Christ. We pray and live the prayer of St. Paul that Mary our Mother is always offering to her Son through His Holy Spirit:

> All I want is to know Christ and the power of His resurrection and to share His sufferings by reproducing the patterns of His death (Ph 3:10).

APPENDIX

Russian Devotion to Mary,
The Mother of God

There is an ancient Russian legend that runs thus: St. Andrew, the Apostle, hurried to heaven, released by his crucifixion from earthly toil and anguish. St. Paul would have called him "The fool for Christ" for he loved the Cross of Our Savior and His Mother at the foot of the Cross. Admitted to the gates of heaven, he began searching for his beautiful heavenly Queen. "Where is she?" he asked his guide. "She's not here," replied the angelic tour master. "She is in the suffering world drying the tears of her weeping children."

Drying their tears, healing their hurts, folding the hands of her suffering children—loving them, looking for them, teaching them, reminding them, praying with them—these are the ways of heaven's Queen on earth, requested by her Son and eagerly followed by His Mother. Christian Russia has treasured the legend of St. Andrew's search for the Mother of God. As patron saint of the Russian people, he can only feel gratitude and consolation that she is on earth helping sufferers. She must, then, be in Russia, where pain has been a daily diet; where Mary has been loved above all earthly creatures since Christianity first came to that land. Christianity has had a long history

in Russia and this history, till lately, has been that of the
Russians wrapped in Mary's mantle.

What sort of a Lady is the Mother of God in the eyes
of the Russians? How did the thousand years of Christianity in Russia represent her? Of old Russia was called
the House of the Mother of God. This was their boast and
glory; and not in vain. Nicholas Berdyaev, one of the
leading modern Russian writers in exile, has gone so far as
to claim religion among Russians as more a religion of
Mary than of Christ. This is of course an exaggeration, but
nevertheless it highlights the important place devotion to
Mary always has occupied among Russians. Of the thousand monasteries in Russia before the Revolution in 1917
more than half were consecrated to Mary. In the Moscow
Patriarchate Church Calendar a partial list of Marian feasts
celebrated yearly in the Russian Orthodox Church is given;
the full list numbers one thousand Marian feasts; several,
that is, for every day in the year.

According to Russian Christianity, nothing in the
Orthodox Church can be achieved without the blessing and
intercession of the Mother of God.

Perhaps the most typical aspect of the Russian's
devotion to the Mother of God is his child-like love for her
and trust in her constant protection and intercession. She
is glorified in Heaven through her Assumption, yet the
Russian finds her presence close to him throughout each
day. She is the Mother of the earthly family of men. A
mother cannot refuse to listen to the child who begs her
help and protection.

THE PROTECTION OF OUR LADY

One of the lesser Byzantine feasts which exalted
Mary's protection of the human race was introduced into
the Russian calendar and has always been ranked in Russia

as one of Mary's great feasts. The Russian's filial confidence toward Our Lady's protection could not help but be drawn to such a feast, called in Russian *Pokrov* or veil. It is celebrated on October 1. The origin of the feast dates back to the ninth century when (the legend says) St. Andrew, the fool for Christ, and his disciple Epiphanius entered the church of Blacherna in Constantinople one evening to assist at Vespers. A majestic Lady appeared to him in a blaze of bright light, accompanied by a cortege of saints, all dressed in white. The Lady passed through the entire church and stopped at the front, praying for a long time and weeping. Finally she raised the large veil which she wore on her head and extended it toward the faithful. The gesture and apparition lasted a long time. So in an allegorical way is commemorated by all Christian Russians on this feast the veil of Mary which she stretches over all humanity as a pledge of her protection and intercession. In the beautiful *tropar* of the Liturgy of that day Mary's earthly children sing: "Cover us with your sacred veil, deliver us from all evil, beg of your Son, Christ our God, that He may save our souls." In the Office for this feast Mary prays to Heaven with suppliant arms uplifted that the burdens of the world may be lightened, that rulers may govern wisely and that our souls may be redeemed. "Christ has given thee to His people as a firm bulwark and protectress to shield and save sinners who fly to thee."

THE SOURCES OF THIS DEVOTION

The two great sources for this tender and fervent devotion toward Mary among Russians are found in their sacred icons and the liturgical texts, always sung during the Divine Liturgy or other liturgical functions in the Russian Rite. I would like first to develop some key ideas about Russian devotion to Mary through veneration of her icons.

Among no other people is the holy image of Mary honored with more reverence and devotion. Mention has already been made of the thousand sacred and miraculous icons honored in the Russian Church. To understand this particular devotion to a painting, one has to understand the psychology of the Oriental Christian.

WHAT IS AN ICON?

Just what then is an icon? An icon is a religious painting of Christ, God, Our Lady, or of other saints, angels, or biblical scenes. But for the Oriental Christian it is not a portrait. It in no way seeks to represent the subject in a realistic, natural form, as for example, the Blessed Mother as she lived on earth. An icon is first of all a channel of grace, a point of contact made between the praying Christian and the heavenly person represented. A blessed icon makes it possible for the suppliant to rise through this visible representation of an invisible person to the spiritual presence of that person.

The icon is the place where Christ appears to us; it is our prayerful meeting point of contact with Him. Praying before an icon, we pray directly to Him; kissing it, we kiss Him; bowing low before it, we bow before Him.

In an icon of Our Lady, if Mary's hands and body do not have the proportions of other women, it makes little difference. The artist seeks to represent, as far as a graphic medium can, the spirituality of the person. The suppliant kneeling before her image is moved by the spirituality expressed in her image and through this rises to her real presence.

THE BLESSING OF AN ICON

The Eastern Rite Ritual gives the following prayer in the ceremony of the blessing of an icon: "O Lord, Our

God, send down the grace of Thy Holy Spirit upon this icon. . .bless it and make it holy. . .grant to it the power and strength of miraculous deeds. Make it a spring of recovery and healing."

Icon painting is not merely an art; it is a prayer, accompanied by fasting and prayer on the part of the artist. He approaches his art only after Confession and Communion. He realizes that God will use this instrument as a channel of grace. St. John Damascene has written a beautiful treatise on icon devotion in the Oriental Church. He sums it all up in the words: "What is seen sanctifies our thoughts and so they fly towards the unseen Majesty of God."

NOT ABSTRACT BUT VISUAL PIETY

The people of Russia, the good, the little people, for centuries fed their hearts with piety through their eyes and ears. Their icons of Christ, of Mary, of the saints and of the angels taught the great truths of Christianity and enabled these truths to live in a sensible form. For centuries the Russian people had no other book than icons, no other words for prayer and study than their Liturgy.

The beauty and the attributes of the Mother of God were told to them as they knelt before her sacred images in humble, suppliant prayer and as they worshiped in the Sacred Liturgy.

Miraculous icons were carried to Russia from Constantinople and they were reproduced in Russia from originals abroad. Often a spiritual revolution took place in some locality when Our Lady miraculously appeared or wrought some miracle. Churches were built to house miraculous icons. Monasteries of men and women often grouped around to honor them fitly.

All this is one large reason why Russia became the
land of the Mother of God.

RUSSIA REMAINED UNCHANGED

Russia stayed for centuries in her illiteracy and
isolation. Communications with Constantinople were generally not frequent. Furthermore, in the fourteenth century hordes of Mongols swept down on Kiev, totally
cutting off Russian contact with the Byzantine center. But
in their seclusion the Russians clung tenaciously to their
precious heritage.

ICONS ARE STILL THE SAME

A Russian artist, painting Our Lady even now, is not
free to yield to inspiration, much as did Raphael or
Rubens, but must observe certain rules and canons. Like a
good poet observing strict rules about metrics and rhymes
who is still capable of breathing into his work individuality
and freshness, so a good iconographer has room for
expansion, but always within the framework of tradition.

In 1551 the Tzar Ivan IV and the Metropolitan of
Moscow, Macarius, called the Council of Stoglav which
prescribed rules about the art of icon painting. Artists were
bound to follow the ancient models of the Greek-
Byzantine artists. Details of the art were minutely speci-
fied in this Council as to preparation of colors, manner of
applying the gilding and so forth. Guides for painting were
books giving the traditional types of how to depict Gospel
scenes or saints. A verbal portrait of the Holy Virgin is
found in one of these guides: "Of middle age, of stature
taller than usual, according to certain witnesses, blonde

beautiful, with black eyebrows, a round, oval face. Long arms, delicate fingers. She shows forth inconceivable beauty through her natural purity and complete humility."

MANY TYPES OF ICONS

To understand properly the Russians' devotion to Mary one must understand the main types of icons depicting Mary. These icons are distinguished by the various prayerful attitudes or poses of Our Lady. One type of the praying Virgin similar to those found in the Roman catacombs shows her with hands lifted in a gesture of prayer. The praying attitude where Mary is depicted alone interceding for men is called the *Pokrov* or veil type because of the original feast of Pokrov which pictures Our Lady praying alone as she extends over the human race her veil, a symbol of her protecting love.

The other praying icon of Mary portrays her with the Infant Jesus. Except for the above mentioned Pokrov type, all the other icon attitudes show Mary with her Divine Son. For the Russian this was the most natural portrait, for is not the most Holy Virgin the way to Jesus, the bridge, the ladder of Jacob bringing earth to heaven and heaven to earth? This second type of praying Virgin is called the *Znamenie* or apparition which shows Mary with the Infant Jesus who is either blessing or has His arms extended in the form of a cross or is being lifted in a prayerful attitude, similar to that of the Mother. The most famous icon of this type is the Virgin of Novgorod which is renowned for the many times it saved the city from destruction. In the seige of the city by the armies of Souzdal, the bishop of Novgorod put the icon on the wall of the city. The enemy rained a cloud of arrows over the wall, one striking the image of the Virgin. The Virgin

turned her eyes toward the enemies with a look of pity
and tears poured from her eyes. In the same instant the
Novgorodians repulsed the enemy.

A SECOND TYPE OF ICON

Besides the praying icons of Mary there is the
Hodiguitria, or the Virgin who points out the way to us
heaven-bound travelers. Mary is pictured holding the
Infant on her arm, generally the left, and with the right
hand pointing to Jesus, inviting through this gesture all of
her earthly children to come to Him. It is a gesture of
tender humility, of effacement, but also a gesture of
mediation. The Kazan and Smolensk icons are famous
examples of this. The Smolensk icon is supposed to have
been a copy of an original painting done by St. Luke for
the Christian Community at Antioch. From there it passed
to Jerusalem, then to Constantinople. The Greek princess
Anna carried it to Russia when she married the Russian
prince Vsevolod. It was carried to battle in the war of
1812 when Smolensk was delivered and has been reproduced everywhere in monasteries and churches. The Kazan
icon is perhaps the most popular among the people. Each
marriage was blessed with a copy of this icon and each
bride carried it into her new home. Children were
dedicated to Mary before this icon; in their sicknesses the
mother and family knelt before this image of Mary and
prayed for a cure. Sons leaving for army service were
blessed by Our Lady through this image.

A THIRD TYPE OF ICON

The third type of Marian icon is called the
Oumilienie, the Virgin of Tenderness. She holds on her

arm her Divine Infant, but He has about Him an almost impish look as He presses close to His Mother, His cheek against hers. It is the most "human" of the Russian icons where maternal and filial sentiment are visibly portrayed. Whoever accuses Russian icons of being too stiff and cold shows he has not studied the icon of Tenderness.

The Vladimir Virgin is the most famous example of this type. It is perhaps the most famous in the history of Russia, dating back to the twelfth century. Before this icon the tzars were crowned and the patriarchs of the Russian Orthodox Church were consecrated. Up to 1919 it was found in the Cathedral of the Assumption inside the Kremlin, but it is now in the Moscow Tretiakov Art Gallery. What emotions must pass through pious, believing Russians as they gaze upon this beloved icon which was synonymous with their Russian homeland and Christian culture up to the Revolution. May they see very soon the return of the Virgin of Vladimir to her exalted position as patroness of Moscow and of all Russia.

The fourth type of icon is a familiar one to us in the West who know it as the icon of Our Lady of Perpetual Help. This type in Russian is called the *Strastnaia*, the Virgin of Sorrows, or the Virgin of the Passion. Jesus is always on the arm of Mary, but turns His gaze away from her in a look of fright toward two angels who appear on high carrying the instruments of His future Passion. The artist is mainly interested in depicting the sorrow of her Son, but every Russian artist painting this icon has succeeded also in depicting with supreme delicateness the sorrow in the countenance of the Divine Mother at the vision of the cross and the lance. The original icon has been attributed to St. Luke. The Russian icon and that of the West of Our Lady of Perpetual Help are copies, varying slightly in style, but retaining the basic *Hodiguitria* or conductor attitude of the Virgin informing about the approaching Passion of Christ.

THE LAST TYPE OF ICON

The last general type of Virgin icon is called the *Deisis*, a group portrait in which Christ is the principal figure. Mary is at His right side with John the Baptist, His Precursor, at His left, the two privileged creatures least unworthy of Him.

NATIONAL PATRONESS OF ALL POLAND

One icon which well shows how the Russians' love for Mary in any image is respected and transcends national prejudices is that of the Virgin of Czestochowa, national patroness of all Poland. Again St. Luke is supposed to have originated it. (With all the icons attributed to St. Luke, both in the East and the West, one wonders how he ever found time to do anything else but paint!) St. Helena carried it from Jerusalem to Constantinople where it remained for five centuries. In 1813 the Tzar, Alexander I, placed a copy of this icon in the Cathedral of Kazan at St. Petersburg, where it was honored annually as a Russian feast on March 6.

A LATIN ICON

There is, too, evidence of Russians' love for Mary's image even when produced in a Western tradition. There is the devotion of St. Seraphim of Sarov to his Latin icon of the Virgin, "Joy of all Joys." Russians love to tell his legend. With the oil which burned before this icon he worked many cures. In 1831 Mary appeared to him, resplendent in celestial glory. She promised to watch over the convent he founded. One day shortly after, he was found dead. The monk in the next room had smelled cloth burning. Rushing in, he saw St. Seraphim still kneeling erect before his image of the Joy of all Joys. The candle he had been holding in his hand had fallen into his habit and ignited the sleeve. Seraphim had gone to meet his Heavenly Joy, the Queen he loved and served so faithfully during his very holy life.

TWO RECENT OCCURRENCES

Two interesting, twentieth century developments in Russia show that this traditional love of Russians toward Our Lady has not been in vain, but that Mary still is watching over her children. One is the discovery of an ancient long-forgotten icon of Our Lady in 1917, the year of the Fatima apparitions. On March 2, in the village of Kolomansk near Moscow, there was discovered this for-gotten icon showing the Mother of God as Queen of the Universe. She is represented as seated on a royal throne, dressed in regal robes, crowned with a precious bejeweled crown and holding in her hands a scepter and a globe. She affectionately presses to her bosom her Divine Son Jesus. This apparition of the royal icon caused a vast and profound religious movement. Innumerable copies were distributed throughout Russia. How many private homes still retain these duplicates, carefully kept out of sight of Soviet investigators, only God and His Mother know.

The other development was reported recently in the Vatican City newspaper *Osservatore Della Domenica.* In many parts of Russia, ancient venerated icons have suddenly and mysteriously become new and fresh. Surfaces dulled by the passing centuries have taken on new luster; cracked paint and wood have been restored. Some incidents have baffled the Soviet police and have led to a religious resurrection among the people. One incident which still is remembered by both the people and the police happened in the small village of Krolevitz, near Vladivostok. An old painting of Christ which hung on the wall of the dark smokey hut of a peasant suddenly appeared new again. The peasants spread word about the village of the "miracle." Soviet police quickly stepped in to settle this religious fanaticism. A bayonet ripped the picture from the wall and feverish hands tore it to shreds. But immediately, before the eyes of the Soviet police, the scattered pieces on the floor came together, making the picture whole again and as new. The police confiscated the picture to prevent spreading such old wives' tales.

LITURGICAL DEVOTION TO THE MOTHER OF GOD

In the Divine Liturgy and in other liturgical functions the Eastern Christian has always been fed with solid theological teaching about the Mother of God, expressed in music and poetry that is unrivaled for splendor and richness. When, prior to his Baptism in 988, Prince Vladimir's legates returned from their trip to Constantinople to investigate the Greek Rite, they reported about the celebration of the Byzantine Liturgy: "We did not know if we were in heaven or on earth, for there is not upon earth such a beautiful spectacle. We have no words to describe it. We can only say that God dwells there with them and their cult is above that of all other lands. We can never forget that beauty."

This beautiful religious rite opened up to the Russian people a filial love for the Mother of God which they carried away from their temples of worship into their everyday lives, into their homes, into their social activities. In the daily Liturgy of the Russians she was constantly being hailed as "Most holy, Most pure, Most blessed and glorious Lady, the Mother of God and ever Virgin Mary."

At this epoch devotion to the Mother of God had blossomed to its fullest. The Eastern Church had seen the gigantic struggle about the mystery of the Trinity, the whole bitter struggle with the Christological adversaries and the many who denied one or more of the privileges of the Mother of God. But after all this St. John Damascene and St. Theodore the Studite transferred all of the theology and the teachings of the Holy Fathers along with the spirit of penitence of the monks to the sphere of Liturgy. St. John Chrysostom, St. Basil, and St. Gregory transferred their penetrating theology and poetry to the Liturgies of the Byzantine Rite that exist unchanged to this day. St. Ephraim, the poet without equal, who sang so eloquently of Mary, is said to have handed down to posterity three million verses in her honor.

SOME PRAYERS FROM THE LITURGY

One of the most beautiful hymns ever composed to honor Our Lady is sung daily in the Byzantine Liturgy: "It is indeed proper to bless thee, Mother of God, the eternally blessed and completely sinless one and the Mother of Our God. Higher in honor than the Cherubim and incomparably more glorious than the Seraphim, who without harm to thy virginity didst give birth to the Word of God; we thee extol, true Mother of God."

Her remembrance is ever before the priest and congregation during the Liturgy. When the priest begins his personal preparation, he stands before the iconostasis or screen which separates the altar from the nave and asks Mary's help in the celebration of the coming mysteries. At the "proskomidia" or preparatory rite of the prosphora or small loaf of bread, in honor of Our Lady he addresses her, saying: "To the honor and memory of our most Blessed Lady, the Mother of God and ever-Virgin Mary, through whose prayers do Thou, O Lord, accept this sacrifice upon Thine own altar in heaven."

MARIAN FEASTS AND PRAYERS

Her feasts were looked forward to with great joy. The Nativity of Mary, the Presentation, Christmas, Annunciation and the Assumption were special days of celebration in the homes of all Eastern Christians.

To better prepare for the great feast of her glorification, her Assumption, a two-weeks' fast was observed. On her other second greatest feast, that of the Annunciation, no one was permitted to work. There was the pious belief that even the birds stopped in building their nests in order to praise the Mother of God on this great feast. The Russians wanted all creatures on this day to join them in singing the glories and praises of their *Bogoroditsa*, Mother of God. And thus was introduced the beautiful custom of giving liberty on this day to little caged birds in order that they may carry to the heavenly throne of the Virgin the joy of the children on earth. In the large cities of Russia carts of these birds arrived. The cages were opened after the celebration of the Divine Liturgy and the little birds took to the heavens amid the cries of children and the emotion of their elders.

VARIED PRAYERS

Marian prayers for her special feasts or special liturgical functions outside of the usual Divine Liturgy are found in the liturgical books called *Menea*, *Oktoich*, *Triodi*, *Akathistnik*, *Euchologion* and the *Moleben*. The *Moleben* is a short petitional service to Christ, the Virgin Mary or some particular saint or to the angels. Often Russians would request this to be sung by the priest after the Divine Liturgy before one of the church's Marian icons, to obtain a favor through her intercession or to return thanks for a grace received from her.

The Akaphist is a much longer service in Mary's honor which was originally composed on the occasion of the liberation of Constantinople from its enemies in the seventh century. Church history tells us that on this occasion there was so much joy that all Constantinople flocked to the Church of Our Lady and sang hymns all night to her in thanksgiving; hence the Greek title meaning "not sitting down." In this Marian service, her whole earthly life is mirrored through the poetry of the author who dwells on each Marian Gospel scene and, using highly colorful metaphors, addresses the Mother of God with the beginning word "Rejoice." Each image adds its own beauty to the fast-moving crescendo of epithets. An example of this is the first *ikos* taken from the Akaphist of Our Lady.

The Angel, sent by God from heaven to say to the Mother of God:

'Rejoice,' seeing Thee, O Lord, become Incarnate, trembled as he stood before her; then he greeted her: 'Rejoice, Thou through whom joy will shine forth. Rejoice, through whom the curse will be dissolved. Rejoice through whom freedom from Adam's fall is won. Rejoice, Thou who driest the tears of Eve. Rejoice, Thou, the height surpassing man's comprehension. Rejoice, depth not fathomed even by Angels. Rejoice for Thou art the throne that supports the King. Rejoice for Thou bearest Him who bears all creation. Rejoice, O Star, preceding the dawn. Rejoice womb in which God becomes Man. Rejoice through whom all creatures find new Life. Rejoice, through whom we adore our Creator. Rejoice, Bride yet ever Virgin.'

TITLES OF MARY

In the various other books containing Marian prayers we find such titles as: Destruction of Hell, Treasure of Purity, More Sublime Than Paradise, Foundation of Earth, Living Paradise, Revealer of the Angelic Life, Chosen Above all the Generations of Humans, More Sublime Than all Things Celestial and Terrestial, The Lord Found Thee As a Flower in the Valley of Corrupted Life, Gariel Was Struck By the Beauty of Thy Virginity and Thy Shining Purity, Thou Who Are Inexpressibly Pure.

It was from such liturgical texts that the Eastern Christians were inspired to name their icons with epithets, each rivaling the other for beauty and showing tender filial devotion to the Mother of God. Each icon was blessed and solemnly given a special title. We find such titles snatched up from the liturgical texts which the people heard in the church services on Mary's feasts: Undying Flower, Indestructible Wall, Rescuer of the Perishing, Prompt to Hear, Joy of all Afflicted, Life-Giving Fountain, Sweet-Smelling Flower, Humility Incarnate, Deliveress From Evil, Joy That Knows No End, Tenderness, Joy of Joys.

MARY – QUEEN

The deep humility and simplicity of the Eastern Christian people showed itself not only in their filial love for and confidence in Mary's powerful protection and intercession, but also in their devotion to her under the title of Queen. We have nearly sixty-five popular prayers found in the eleven larger Marian feasts and on the days which celebrate the more famous of the numerous icons of Mary. Over and over she is addressed as the Lady or as the Sovereign Queen. The ingenuity of the authors of these prayers is never exhausted in finding new variations such as: Queen of Heaven and Earth; Most Merciful and Wise Queen of the Saving Light and Mother of the King, Christ Our God; Queen of all Queens; Venerable and Most Mercifully Sweet Queen and Mistress, Chosen From Among all Races and Praised by all Generations, Both Celestial and Terrestial.

CHRISTMAS

For the Greek or Slav Christians, Mary is the most precious finite gift God has given us. And when he is at a loss as to what to offer God as a befitting gift, he turns to his Heavenly Queen. The beautiful hymn sung at Christmas clearly shows this loving attitude toward Mary:

> What shall we bring to Thee, Christ, who this day has appeared on our earth as Man for us? All Thy other creatures bring something to Thee this day: angels, heavenly song; the heavens, the stars; the Wisemen, gifts; the shepherds, wonderment; the earth, a cave; the desert, a crib; and we, we offer the Virgin Mother.

FOOTNOTES

Chapter 1

[1]Tertullian: *De Carne Christi*; Cap. 17; *PL.* 2; 782A-C.

[2]*Sermones Exegetici*; in: *Opera omnia latine et syriace*; Vol. 2 (Rome, 1740) p. 327.

[3]*De Fide Orthodoxa*, 4, 14; *PG.* 94; 1161A

[4]*4.2 Dorm.* 3; *PG.* 96; 728B.

[5]*Lumen Gentium*, #58.

[6]*Ibid.*, #53.

[7]Mk 3:31-35; Lk 11:27-28; 2:41-51; 23:49, 55; Mk 15:40-41; Jn 19:25; Mt 27:55.

[8]*Lumen Gentium*, #58.

[9]*Ibid.*, #61.

[10]These ideas are more fully developed in: *Woman Is the Glory of Man* by E. Danniel and B. Olivier (Westminster, 1966).

[11]L. Beirnaert: *Mystique et continence* (Paris, 1952) p. 377.

[12]C. G. Jung: *Answer to Job* (Cleveland and N.Y., 1954) pp. 192-195.

[13]*Ibid.*, pp. 198-200.

[14]Epiphanius: *Panarion* LXXVIII, cap. 18-19; *PG.* XLII; 729.

[15]Gerhoh of Reichersberg: *Liber de gloria Filii hominis*, 10; *PL.* 194; 1105. Quoted by H. Rahner: *Our Lady—the Church* (Chicago, Ill. 1965) pp. 55-56.

Chapter 2

[1] E. Neumann: *Origins and History of Consciousness* (Princeton, 1971) p. 121.

[2] See the presentation of three schools of exegesis concerning Mary's virginity in: E. Schillebeeckx: *Mary, Mother of the Redemption* (N.Y., 1964) pp. 56-59.

[3] K. Rahner: *Mary Mother of the Lord* (N.Y., 1963) pp. 63-72.

[4] *N.J.B.*, Jn. 1:13; cf. footnotes k. and l.

[5] For a detailed examination of this matter, cf. F. M. Braun, O.P.: "Qui ex Deo natus est (Jean 1:13)" in: *Aux Sources de la tradition chrétienne.* Mélanges offerts à M. Maurice Goguel (Paris, 1950) pp. 11-13. Also his book: *Mother of God's People* (Staten Island, N.Y., 1967) pp. 35-45.

Chapter 3

[1] St. John Damascene: *l Adversus Nestorium*, 1; *PG.* 95, 189A.

[2] Cf. St. Maximus the Confessor: *Ambigua*; *PG.* 91; 1304D-1305C.

[3] St. Irenaeus: *Adversus Haereses*; V,21, 1; pp. 548-549. (*The Ante-Nicene Fathers* Vol. IV; ed. by A. Roberts and J. Donaldson; Grand Rapids, Mich., 1962).

[4] St. Athanasius: *De Incarnatione et Contra Arianos*; *PG.* 26, 5; 992.

[5] L. Bouyer: *The Seat of Wisdom* (N.Y., 1960) pp. 146-148.

[6] St. Justin: *Dialogue with Trypho*, cap. 100, *PG.* 6; 709-712.

[7] For various aspects of Irenaeus' theory of recapitulation cf: A.d'Ales: "La doctrine de la récapitulation en Saint Irénée;" in: *Recherches de science religieuse*; Vol. 6, 1916; pp. 185-211.

[8] St. Irenaeus: *Adversus Haereses*; Lib. III, cap. 22, 1; Harvey, W. W., (Cambridge, 1857); Vol. 2; pp. 123-124. *PG.* 958B-960.

[9]*Adversus Haereses*; Lib. V, cap. 19, 1; Harvey, 2, p. 375-376. *PG.* 7: 1175A-1176A. Other texts: *Ibid*; Lib. III, 21, 10; *PG.* 7: 954C-955B. Lib. III, 18, 7; *PG.* 7; 938AB; *Ibid*: 1245B. *Demonstratio Apostolicae Praedicationis*; cap. 33; *Patrol. Orient.* Vol. 12, pp. 684-685.

[10]St. Epiphanius: *Panarion* LXXVIII, cap. 18-19; *PG.* 42; 729.

[11]*Ibid.*, 733 ss.

[12]Quoted in: P. Palmer: *Mary in the Documents of the Church* (Westminster, Md., 1952) p. 60.

[13]*Ibid.*, p. 22.

[14]*Ibid.*, p. 51.

[15]*Ibid.*, p. 58.

[16]*Ibid.*, p. 23.

[17]*Ibid.*, p. 50.

[18]*Ibid.*, p. 54.

[19]*Ibid.*, p. 25.

[20]*Mariology*; ed. Juniper B. Carol (Milwaukee, 1957) Vol. 1; p. 187.

Chapter 4

[1]L. Cerfaux: *Introduction`a la Bible* T. II; p. 339. Cf: Acts 1:1-2 and Lk 1:1-4.

[2]Cf. J. Audet: "L'Annonce `a Marie" in: *Revue Biblique*, 63 (1956) pp. 346-374.

[3]*In Gen.* hom. III, 7; *Sources Chrétiennes*, Vol. 7, p. 123.

[4]*In Cant. Cantic.* hom. II, 6; *Sources Chrétiennes*, Vol. 37, p. 91.

[5]Dr. Irene Claremont de Castillejo: *Knowing Woman* (Harper-Colophon, N.Y. 1973).

[6] St. Augustine: *Confessions*; Book X, 6.

[7] St. John Damascene: *l Dormitio*, 10; *PG.* 96; 716C.

Chapter 5

[1] *L.G.* II 56.

[2] *L.G.* II 53.

[3] Karl Rahner: *Mary Mother of the Lord* (N.Y. 1963) p. 49.

[4] J. H. Newman: *An Essay on the Development of Christian Doctrine* (Garden City, N.Y. 1962).

[5] Cf.: J. H. Walgrave: *Newman the Theologian* (N.Y. 1960) p. 174.

[6] Tertullian: *Contra Celsum: De Spectaculis*; cap. XXX; *PL.* 1; 6626.

[7] Irenaeus: *Adversus Haereses*; V; 19, 1; *PG.* 7; 1175.

[8] Tertullian: *De Carne Christi*; VII; *PL.* 2; 766. Cf. also: *Adversus Marcionem*; IV, 19; *PL.* 2.

[9] Origen: *In Lucam*; *Homilia XVII*; *PG.* 13; 1845; *Homilia XIX*; 1849B.

[10] St. Cyril: *In Joannem*; XII; *PG.* 74; 661B-664A.

[11] *Ibid.*

[12] St. John Chrysostom: *Homilia IV in Matt.*, 5; *PG.* 57; 45.

[13] St. John Chrysostom: *Homilia XXI in Joan.* 2; *PG.* 59; 130.

[14] St. John Chrysostom: *Homilia XLIV in Matt.* 1; *PG.* 57; 464-465.

[15] Cf.: S. Bulgakov: *The Orthodox Church* (London, 1935) p. 138.

[16] St. Cyril of Jerusalem: *Catecheses XVII*, 6; *PG.* 33; 976.

[17] St. Ephrem: *Sermo Adversus Hereticos*; in: *Opera omnia graece et latine*; Vol. 2 (Rome, 1743) p. 270.

[18]St. Epiphanius: *Panarion LXXVIII*, 18; *PG.* 42; 728.

[19]St. Ephrem: *Hymni de beata Maria*; XIII, no. 5, 6 (Lamy) Vol. 2; p. 577.

[20]St. Ephrem: *Carmina Nisibena*; XXVII; ed. G. Bickell (Leipzig, 1866) p. 122.

[21]Cf.: G. Jouassard: "Marie à travers la patristique. Maternité divine, virginité, sainteté; in: Collection: *Maria*; Vol. I (Paris, 1949) pp. 101-104.

[22]St. Ambrose: *Expositio in Ps. CXVIII*; Sermo XXII, no. 30; *PL.* 15; 1599.

[23]St. Augustine: *De Natura et Gratia*; Cap. XXXVI, no. 42; *PL.* 44; 267.

[24]St. Augustine: *Opus Imperfectum*; Lib. IV, cap. 122; *PL.* 45; 1418.

[25]J. H. Newman: *Certain Difficulties Felt by Anglicans in Catholic Teaching* (London, 1876) pp. 31 ss.

[26]Pseudo-Dionysius: *De Caelesti Hierarchia*; X, 1; *De Ecclesiastica Hierarchia* VI, 6: *PG.* 3; 272; 537.

[27]Cf.: J. M. Jugie: "Saint André de Crète et l'immaculée conception," in: *Echos d'Orient*; t. XIII (1910) p. 129.

[28]St. Andrew of Crete: *In Nativitate B. Mariae*; Homil. I; *PG.* 97; 812.

[29]St. Andrew of Crete: *In Dormitionem B. Mariae*; Homil. I; *PG.* 97; 1068.

[30]St. Andrew of Crete: *In Nativitate B. Mariae*; *PG.* 97; 872.

Chapter 6

[1]For a detailed discussion of the term, *woman*, in these three contexts of the Johannine writings cf.: F. M. Braun, O.P.: *Mother of*

God's People (Staten Island, 1967) pp. 50-168 and L. Deiss: *Mary–Daughter of Sion* (Collegeville, Minn. 1972) pp. 129-198.)

[2]T. Koehler: "Maternité spirituelle de Marie," in *Maria, Etudes sur la Vierge*, I (Paris, 1949) p. 583.

Chapter 7

[1]Ticonius: *Regulae*; *PL.* 18; 33, 46, quoted by H. DeLubac: *The Splendour of the Church* (N.Y. 1955) pp. 264-265.

[2]*Lumen Gentium*, #53.

[3]*Ibid.*

[4]St. Augustine: *De S. Virginitate* 6; *PL.* 40, 399.

[5]Quoted by H. Koch: *Virgo Eva–Virgo Maria* (Berlin-Leipzig, 1937) p. 42.

[6]Clement of Alexandria: *Paedagogus*, I, 6; *PG.* 8, 300B.

[7]St. Didymus of Alexandria: *De Trinitate*; II, 13; *PG.* 39, 692A-B.

[8]St. Gregory of Nyssa: *De Virginitate*; II; *PG.* 46, 324B.

[9]St. Augustine: *Confessions*, IV, 12, 19; *PL.* 32, 701.

[10]St. Augustine: *Sermo Denis*; XXV, 8, Morin; p. 163, quoted by A. Müller: *Ecclesia-Maria, die Einheit Marias und der Kirche* (Fribourg, 1951) p. 191.

[11]St. Augustine: *De S. Virginitate*, VI; *PL.* 40, 399.

[12] *Ibid.*

[13]H. Urs von Balthasar: "Wer is die Kirche?" in: *Sponsa Verbi: Skizzen zur Theologie II* (Einsiedeln, 1961) p. 168.

[14]*L.G.* #60.

[15]*L.G.* #61.

[16] Heribert Mühlen, S.J.: *Una Mystica Persona*, 3rd ed. (Paderborn, 1968) p. 492.

[17] *Ibid.*, p. 460.

[18] *L.G.* #62.

Chapter 8

[1] St. John Damascene: *Homily III on the Dormition*; *PG.* 96; 757 B.C.).

[2] L. Bouyer: "Le Culte de Marie dans la liturgie byzantine," in *Maison-Dieu*, (1954) p. 38.

[3] I am indebted in this part to D. Flanagan and his ideas expressed in his article: "Eschatology and Assumption," in: *Concilium*, Vol. 41 (N.Y. 1967) pp. 135-146.

[4] *L.G.* #68.

[5] B. J. LeFrois: *The Woman Clothed with the Sun* (Rome, 1954) p. 262.

Chapter 9

[1] *L.G.* #50.

[2] Q. E. Schillebeeckz, O.P.: *Mary Mother of the Redemption* (N.Y. 1964) pp. 146-162.